PROBLEMS OF
BRITISH ECONOMIC
POLICY 1870–1945

PROBLEMS OF
BRITISH ECONOMIC
POLICY 1870–1945

—— ◇ ——

Jim Tomlinson

METHUEN

LONDON and NEW YORK

First published in 1981 by
Methuen & Co. Ltd
11 New Fetter Lane, London EC4P 4EE

Published in the USA by
Methuen & Co.
in association with Methuen, Inc.
733 Third Avenue, New York, NY 10017

© 1981 Jim Tomlinson

Printed in Great Britain by
Richard Clay (The Chaucer Press) Ltd
Bungay, Suffolk

British Library Cataloguing in Publication Data
Tomlinson, Jim
Problems of British economic policy, 1870–1945.
1. Great Britain – Economic conditions –
19th century
2. Great Britain – Economic conditions –
20th century
3. Great Britain – Economic policy
I. Title
330.941'081   HC255   80–41942

ISBN 0–416–30430–3
ISBN 0–416–30440–0 Pbk (University paperback 740)

Acknowledgements

I am grateful to Dudley Baines, Malcolm Falkus and David Higham for comments on particular parts of this book. The general approach of the book owes a great deal to discussions in the Conference of Socialist Economists 'Money Group' with Stuart Burchell, David Fishman, Grahame Thompson and, above all, Athar Hussain. Chris Newnham typed the manuscript with her customary speed and efficiency.

I should also like to thank The Macmillan Press and St Martin's Press, Inc. for permission to reproduce table 2.1, p.40 and Professor E.V. Morgan for permission to reproduce table 7.1, p.109.

Contents

Introduction:
Approaches to economic policy

In the title of this book the stress is on the word 'problems' for two separate but related reasons. Firstly, the major purpose in writing this book has been to raise a range of problems about the way in which economic policy decisions are discussed in the literature. Thus, although the book takes a roughly chronological form, the areas discussed have been chosen primarily for the materials they offer for the raising of these problems. Inevitably this means that the book is *not* a comprehensive textbook of British economic policy over the 1870–1945 period. Many areas are omitted, not only for reasons of space but also because they do not seem to offer the same potential for raising problems as the ones I have chosen.

Secondly, I have stressed 'problems' because I have been at pains to construct the argument that the way in which areas of economic policy become 'problems' for policy makers is always problematic, that it is never obvious and never happens 'naturally'. This approach contrasts with that adopted in many economics textbooks where the objects of policy are treated more or less as given, and the discussion then becomes one of how these pre-given objects are reconciled. Typical is Shaw's book[1]* which lists full employment, price stability, economic growth, a satisfactory balance of payments and regional balance as macroeconomic policy objectives in Britain today. Practically no space is given to discussing for whom these problems exist, how they came to exist, and what the conditions of existence of such policy objectives are. These are precisely the kinds of questions I shall devote attention to in this book.

*Notes are to be found at the end of the book.

I

For purposes of exposition we can schematically divide general characterizations of economic policy into three – Keynesian, Marxist and neoclassical. In so far as recent discussions of British economic policy have had an explicit general theory as a framework, this has been predominantly a Keynesian one. This is particularly true of the literature on twentieth-century economic policy,[2] though it is apparent also in writings on earlier periods.[3] The Keynesian position could be said to have as its motto one of the most often quoted passages from Keynes's *General Theory of Employment, Interest and Money*:

> the ideas of economists and political philosophers, both when they are right and when they are wrong, are more powerful than is commonly understood. Indeed the world is ruled by little else. Practical men, who believe themselves to be quite exempt from any intellectual influences, are usually the slave of some deficient economist. Madmen in authority, who hear voices in the air, are distilling their frenzy from some academic scribbler of a few years back. I am sure that the power of vested interests is vastly exaggerated compared with the gradual encroachment of ideas. Not, indeed, immediately but after a certain interval; for in the field of economic and political philosophy there are not many who are influenced by new theories after they are twenty-five or thirty years of age, so that the ideas which civil servants and politicians and even agitators apply to current events are not likely to be the newest. But, soon or late, it is ideas, not vested interests, which are dangerous for good or evil.[4]

In this way Keynes brought to the centre of the discussion of economic policy a simple dichotomy – ideas versus vested interests. Whilst not originating it, Keynes inserted this dichotomy into particular policy discussions and gave it a new cutting edge. Ever since, Keynesians have tended to draw from this a stress on economic theory as a determinant of economic policy.[5] Winch, for example, whilst outlining objections to a conception of a close relation between economic theory and economic policy is drawn into implying in many cases just such a relation. Firstly because of the organization of his text around the question 'what were economists saying about such and such a policy question', and secondly because the alternative is seen as the view 'that the history of economic thought is a history of ideologies, or one that reflects in a straightforward fashion the dominant interest groupings or practical problems of society at any particular time'.[6]

Similarly Howson and Winch at the end of their introduction to the Economic Advisory Council documents[7] explicitly attack Terence Hutchinson[8] who expressed doubts about the importance of economic theory to policy decisions in the 1930s. They support Keynes's statement of 1942 that there were 'few passages in the history of controversy more valuable ... than that which took place among economists in the ten years ... before the war', because they see these theoretical controversies feeding directly into government policy on demand management and unemployment policy at the end of the Second World War.[9] Again Howson's book on monetary management stresses the centrality of the Treasury's theories in determining its policies, its major concern being 'the consequences of the theoretical views held by the Treasury men'.[10]

This conception of the role of economic theory in policy making clearly stems a great deal from a conception of the effects of Keynes's theories on economic policy in the 1930s and 1940s. This conception is looked at in more detail in Chapter 8 below. Here I will make some general comments on this conception of the role of economic theory in making policy. (With its implications of a history of economic policy seen as a reflection, presumably with lags, of a history of economic thought.)

Against this I wish to suggest the contingent and changing nature of the 'problems' which exist for economic policy. These problems (see for example Chapter 1 on Unemployment) are not the creation of economic theory but are the product of a heterogeneous set of elements, both discursive and non-discursive. Economic theory is not 'produced' by these problems, as a reductionist analysis would imply; but even less could it be said that the theory 'creates' the problem. Secondly, the Keynesian position assumes that there is in principle a set of agents (in the Treasury, Bank of England or whatever) who can be seen as the effective controllers of policy. If they can be converted (although Keynes himself appears to have considered this unlikely – see quotation above) to a new theoretical position then policy can be changed. The problem of such a conception can be illustrated by reference to a modern controversy in economic policy. Assume that the Treasury and the government generally became converted to the

Left's 'Alternative Economic Strategy' and therefore accepted the necessity of strict planning agreements to oversee the level of investment in enterprises. Could such a conversion of the policy makers be made effective? Only with a much more difficult and problematic reform of a whole set of institutions – for example trade union practices, management practices, company law relating to disclosure, etc. The reform of the ideology of the Treasury would be a fairly minor component of such a process. Yet the Keynesian position would always tend to highlight this, at the expense of the detailed work and struggle over institutional changes.

This example is meant to illustrate the banal but often neglected point that economic policy is not just constrained by the 'ideology' of the policy makers. All policies have conditions of existence outside the minds of those who determine policy. This argument not only downgrades the role of economic theory in policy making, but equally stresses the importance of the institutional arrangements within which policy is made. The Keynesian position denegates the role of institutions – they are conceived mainly as aids or impediments to the spread of enlightenment, not as having any effectivity of their own. (This denegation of the role of specific institutions is implicit in *any* general conception of policy making: all general theories would be subverted if the specificity of institutional conditions is admitted to matter – see further below.)

The Keynesian position gains a great deal of strength from its insertion in the dichotomy constructed by Keynes: if one doesn't stress the role of theory one is forced into a vested interest argument – policy making is simply a reflection of political power. This dichotomy should itself be problematized by asking if its terms really exhaust the way in which policy can be conceived. I argue below that this is not the case. Nevertheless there is a considerable amount of writing on economic policy which implicitly or explicitly asserts, against Keynes, the centrality of 'interests' in policy decisions. This position could be called the Marxist theory of economic policy, though many writers who are not Marxists subscribe to a version of it.

Marxist writers have rarely produced an extended discussion of economic policy, but the basic position seems a clear one. Mandel, for example, writing about the increased role of the state in the economy argues that

The transition from competitive capitalism to imperialism and monopoly capitalism necessarily altered both the bourgeoisie's subjective attitude towards the state and the objective function fulfilled by the state in the performance of its central tasks.[11]

Thus policy changes are seen as derived from the particular stage reached by capitalism. No mechanism for this derivation is specified by Mandel, but within Marxism this has generally been done, if at all, by conceptualizing political forces as representing the interests of the bourgeoisie, proletariat, etc. This makes possible a conception of capitalism and the bourgeoisie's interests being translated into policy by the action of these political forces − whether it be the Confederation of British Industry (CBI) or the Conservative Party or whatever. As Barry Hindess has pointed out, such conceptions of political forces have brought out a fundamental ambiguity in Marxist discussions of politics.

[Either they] effectively reduce political and ideological phenomena to class interests determined elsewhere (basically in the economy) i.e. an economic reductionism coupled with a vague recognition that things are more complicated and a failure to get to grips with that complication. Or we must face up to the real autonomy of political and ideological forces and phenomena and their irreducibility to manifestations of interests determined by the structure of the economy.[12]

These points are equally valid in relation to the specific question of economic policy making; the orthodox Marxist position implies a reduction of policy to interests which are constituted elsewhere than in the policy making institutions. To revoke the 'relative autonomy' of institutions is merely to evade the problem by a play on words.

The Marxist position, like the Keynesian, necessarily denegates the role of institutions. Institutions are conceived as aids or impediments to the effectiveness of pre-given interests rather than of pre-given theories. Ultimately they are puppets on a string, dancing to the tunes played by capitalists. Such a position is commonly taken by Marxists in discussions of economic policy, both historical and contemporary. Thus Walton and Gamble explain the state's role in the labour market in these instrumentalist terms: 'In 1975 even 3, 4, 5 per cent unemployment does not discipline the labour force and reduce their wage demands. The state is obliged to step in directly to confront the working class on behalf of capital.'[13] The mechanisms whereby capital articulates its interests and is able to subordinate all state agencies to these interests are not explained. In the absence of such explanation this position depends on an article of faith – under capitalism the state *must be* subordinate to the will of capitalists.

A similar, if slightly less crude position is taken by a (non-Marxist) historian like Pollard, who represents the 1925 decision in Britain to return to gold at the pre-war parity as simply reflecting the interests of bankers in the City of London.[14] (On this decision see Chapter 6 below.)

The argument here is not that the notion of interests should be abandoned entirely, but that its use should be carefully circumscribed in explanations of policy. Firstly because conceiving of policy as representing interests evades all the problems associated with the concept of representation (see further below). Secondly because it doesn't face up to the question why do certain interests conceive such and such a policy to be to their advantage. For example to say that current (autumn 1980) economic policies of the Tory government are in the interests of 'business' is made plausible by the CBI's support for these policies. But such an argument leaves unanswered *why* the CBI should conceive high interest rates, a high exchange rate and general deflation to be in their interests when they appear to be creating havoc in firms. Obviously there is some sort of answer, some underlying calculation, but this example surely undercuts any view of policy as straightforwardly and unproblematically representing interests.

In the last two decades a further approach to economic policy making has grown rapidly in the USA, and has been applied to both contemporary and historical materials. This approach can, broadly, be called neoclassical, because it conceptualizes policy making as the result of maximizing behaviour on the part of human agents involved in the government or state agencies. Though such an approach has barely surfaced in discussions of the *history* of British economic policy,[15] it is worth examining this approach briefly not only because it is likely soon to be prevalent in Britain (given British economic history's high propensity to import from the USA) but also because it raises important general problems about frameworks for discussing economic policy.

The neoclassical approach can be seen as a logical extension of the general (neoclassical) definition of economics as, in the words of Robbins, 'the science which studies human behaviour as a relationship between ends and scarce means which have alternative uses'.[16] Clearly there is no logical reason why such an approach should be confined to what is conventionally defined as the *subject matter* of economics — the production and consumption of goods and services. Becker,[17] for example, argues that the concepts of maximizing behaviour, market equilibrium and stable preferences provide an approach, consistent with a Robbins style definition, to *all* human behaviour.

In particular the concept of maximizing behaviour can readily be applied to policy making. Thus Downs[18] constructs a theory in which vote maximizing is made the goal of political parties, and utility maximizing the aim of voters. This generates a whole number of results relating to the political process. A similar mode of analysis can be applied to bureaucracy.[19] From such analyses most British discussions have been concerned to construct implications for government expenditure (in the USA this approach has been much more widely used — for example in discussions of regulation of industry).[20]

In this way there emerges an argument which suggests that governments gain votes from expenditure, due to the unequal distribution of expenditure and tax raising: most spending aids only a few voters whilst the costs are widely distributed. Thus the recipients constantly press for more spending, whilst the tax payers have insufficient incentive to resist. As a result, government expenditure in a democratic system tends to rise.[21] This, it is argued, is reinforced by the attitudes that have replaced the strong commitment to balanced budgets allowing governments to spend without taxing.[22]

Similarly bureaucrats are seen as having a vested interest in the extension of the size of bureaucracies and therefore of government spending.

> As a general rule, a bureaucrat will find that his possibilities for promotion increase, his power, influence and public respect improve, and even the physical conditions of his office improve if the bureaucracy in which he works expands.[23]

The cutting edge of such arguments is often an explicit attack on what is seen as the Keynesian assumption that policy is made by an elite of disinterested, wise and enlightened people. This is counterposed to the assumption that 'politicians respond to pressures emanating from constituents and the state bureaucracy'.[24] Thus the dominance of self-interested motivation is posed as an alternative, more 'realistic' notion to the Keynesian naivety about human motives.[25]

This kind of argument has clearly some similarity to that pursued above about the role of theory in Keynesian conceptions of policy making. The neoclassical position downgrades the role of economic theory, going so far in some cases as to argue that economic theorizing will tend to follow behind the formulation of policies made for other reasons.[26] However, apart from this negative point, the neoclassical framework appears to have little to offer in the analysis of policy making.

The general problem of such analyses can be illustrated initially by reference to the neoclassical theory of the firm, which is probably the cornerstone of such theories. In this framework the firm is conceived as directed by calculations of profit because the shareholders who own the firm have clear financial interest in profitability.

This raises two problems. Firstly, it assumes an unambiguous and unitary conception of profit – without it the theory loses all generality. However, one must be very dubious about such a conception of profit calculation[27] – firms' calculations of 'profit' actually define profit in a variety of different ways, depending on financial, accounting and other exigencies and there is no guarantee that these are reducible to each other. Secondly, the theory assumes some conception of a single locus of control within the enterprise so that calculation is made unambiguously effective.[28] This raises a whole host of problems in relation to the modern firm in which, for example, it is difficult to maintain that the relation between shareholders and managers is simply one of controller and controlled (a fact which has given rise to managerial theories of the firm). But, much more than this, any *general* theory of the firm must imply this notion of a single locus of control so that for every firm we have some way of answering the question 'who controls?' However against this it can be argued that the whole notion of a unitary controlling centre is misplaced and that any firm is a site of multiple struggles over decisions with no single hierarchy of control – to say 'who controls' is impossible.

If we now look at policy making in the light of these points crucial weaknesses (briefly stated) of the neoclassical approach are apparent. Firstly, the *object* of calculation is even more ambiguous in the case of policy – what do policy makers seek to maximize? Usually the answer given is either so general as to be vacuous – 'power' for instance. If it is more specific, perhaps 'votes', the problem is that no obvious kind of calculation emerges from this assumption. One can concede for the sake of argument that politicians seek to maximize their support, but what is of interest is the means that are used to do this, and to this the neoclassical position can provide no general answer. (With the theory of the firm, even if we were to concede that there is an unambiguous notion of profit, it is clear that no necessary consequences result – a *range* of different procedures can be conceived of as those which will be profit maximizing.)

Secondly, the neoclassical conception of policy making, like that of the firm, implies an unambiguous controller of policy who is able to make his calculations effective. As in the case of the firm this can be challenged on the grounds of its implied conception of institutions as 'totalitarian', rather than as conglomerations of diffuse and heterogeneous decision making.

Like the Keynesian and Marxist conceptions of policy making discussed above, the neoclassical conception assumes the possibility of a general theory and, therefore, necessarily denegates the role of institutions. However, this is combined with a notion of the effectivity of institutions in shaping the object of maximization – thus the example of Tullock's argument for introducing competition into bureaucracy.[29] But once it is conceded that institutions shape that which is maximized, the basis of a general theory of calculation is greatly weakened. Then, it is the organization of institutions which matters and the 'general calculating subject' can be displaced by agents who are constructed as effects of that organization. Within the neoclassical framework the resolution of the dilemma between a general theory and the effectivity of institutions in favour of the latter seems unacceptable, but it is the resolution which I have attempted to adopt in this book. I argue that human and other agents engage in calculation, but that this has no general nature, and is the effect of particular institutional arrangements.

If one took, as an example of this line of argument, the 1925 decision to return to the gold standard it could be argued, from a neoclassical perspective, that it was a result of governmental calculations of the way to maximize votes in the next election. This would raise, firstly, the problem of who made this calculation, and how the calculation is guaranteed its effectivity in the making of the decision – an institutional question. Secondly, a postulated motive of vote maximization is an insufficient explanation because it could reasonably be argued that both going back to gold and not going back would be economically and, presumably therefore, electorally advantageous. The choice between the competing options would again depend largely on the way different institutions – the Bank of England, the Treasury, the Cabinet, etc. – conceived of the effects of the gold standard, and this would depend on the precise nature of those institutions.

II

For these kinds of reasons this book eschews *any* general theory of policy making because all such theories denegate the role of institutions. This rejection of *general* theories is not of course an appeal to 'the facts' to somehow correct the inadequacies of theory. Such notions always imply a sleight of hand – the designation of a realm of facts prior to any conceptualization, but facts which necessarily reflect a different order of conceptualization. What follows is based on a *conception* of policy making: it is not an attempt at that conjuring trick which makes the facts 'speak for themselves'. This conception has been outlined in a rather negative way in this introduction because, as it is based on an explicit repudiation of any general theory, its more positive aspects are mainly reserved for the particular discussion in each chapter. Its effects could be summarized as follows.

A major thrust of my argument is to break up the ground on which the 'ideas' versus vested interest dichotomy exists. Approaches to economic policy which work within this duality imply that the objects of policy are obvious. Thus for example Keynesian discussions of the 1930s imply that unemployment becomes an object of policy once mass unemployment exists – the question concerns which theory to bring to bear to solve the problem. The vested interest argument would see objects of policy emerging at the behest of those interests. Against these conceptions I stress the particularity of the objects of policy, their contingent nature, their derivation from political, economic and other conceptions and 'events', their dependence on a range of heterogeneous conditions of existence.

Secondly, and in relation to this I stress the specificity of the institutions involved in policy making. By this is meant, primarily, that there is no general theory which can account for institutions and their practices. Above all this is because a general theory of institutions always seems to imply that institutional practices represent something else – be it ideas, vested interests, the self-interest of those in the institution or whatever. But the whole notion of representation on which such conceptions rely appears insupportable. Any means of representation *necessarily* effects what is represented, except where those means are conceived of as simply a reflection. Once this is conceded then the institution's practices become important because they are not reducible to something else (ideas, interests, etc.)[30]

Thus political arguments about whether institutions (political parties, parliaments) are 'really' representative of their members and constituents have no resolution, because representation has no single meaning.[31] Because of this I take institutional practices seriously in their own terms – as having conditions of existence and effects outside themselves, but not simply as signs of something else.[32]

— 1 —

Unemployment as an object of policy before 1914

Some quantity of unemployment can be considered a necessary accompaniment to the existence of capitalism, in so far as that existence entails labour markets. Labour under capitalism is a commodity distributed through a large number of heterogeneous markets, and there are no means by which the operations of these markets can guarantee a perfect match of the variegated labours employers wish to buy and workers to sell. As Beveridge noted, 'There is nothing in the existing industrial order to secure this miraculously perfect adjustment [of supply and demand for labour].'[1] Unemployment is then inescapable under capitalism, not through any 'inhumanity' or 'irrationality' of the system, but because of the absence of any conceivable institutional means to avoid it. However, the constancy of unemployment's existence under capitalism by no means implies a constancy as an object of policy, such a status always being conditional on particular circumstances.

In the period covered by this book a great range of elements have combined at various times to construct unemployment as a problem of government policy. These have included the cost of unemployment – either in relation to government expenditure on relief measures, or in relation to some conception of the burden on the economy as a whole; unemployment as a cause of pauperism, of moral and physical degeneration; unemployment as a cause of political unrest and violence; unemployment as a sign of uncompetitiveness and impending national decline. These elements are not at par nor are they mutually exclusive. Listing them does, however, serve to illustrate in a general way that this chapter and Chapters 4 and 8 seek to show more specifically: unemployment as an object of policy is constructed out of diverse elements in diverse conjunctures, never simply as a result of 'the fact' of unemployment.

The mass unemployment of the inter-war period is commonly thrown into relief by attempts to contrast the levels of unemployment then prevailing with the levels before 1914. Such comparisons abound with statistical problems. Between the wars the National Insurance figures are the main source of unemployment data, but the system began only in 1911 and initially involved only around 2.25 million workers (July 1914).[2] Before National Insurance there are only the narrowly based trade union figures for small numbers of skilled on which to base estimates and the usefulness of which is therefore largely confined to showing aggregate trends rather than precise percentages.[3] The figures show the absence before 1914 of long periods of unemployment in the staple industries that were hit so hard after 1920, though the comparison is more easily made for engineering, metals and shipbuilding[4] than, for example, in cotton and coal where widespread short-time working complicates the picture.

However, broad comparisons between the pre- and post-war period raise much more than statistical problems. Underlying such comparisons is the notion that there is a common problem 'unemployment' the magnitude of which varies over time. But the unemployment problem for policy makers of the inter-war period is different in kind and not just in degree from the unemployment problem before the First World War. The level of unemployment amongst shipbuilders, miners, cotton workers, etc. is relatively unimportant in discussing policy because it is not with these groups that unemployment policy is largely concerned. Instead unemployment was seen mainly as a problem linked to the casual labourer, classically located in the docks but embracing a vast range of other sectors of service and small scale manufacturing industry particularly in the large cities. So, in discussing policy towards unemployment, comparisons between before and after 1914 can be positively misleading, because they are often based on comparisons of like with unlike.

This may be thought of as a convoluted way of stating the obvious. Miners, cotton workers, shipbuilders, etc. were not unemployed on a large scale for prolonged periods before 1914 and therefore they were not the centre of policy attention. Where is the need for more explanation than this? The answer divides into two. In Chapter 4 below I argue that the unemployment in the staple industries after 1920 became an object of policy as an effect of specific conditions in British economy and society not simply because a lot of people in these industries became unemployed. In this chapter I want to argue that the predominance of casual unemployment in policy making before 1914 was not simply because of widespread casual unemployment; its existence long pre-dated its emergence as a policy problem.[5] The relative lack of significance attached to unemployment in the staple trades at this time reflects not so much the 'low' level of unemployment in these industries as the way unemployment was conceived as a problem. After all much *lower* levels of unemployment than those prevalent before 1914 prompted significant policy changes in the mild recessions which interrupted the boom of the two and a half decades after 1945.

I

Stedman Jones's *Outcast London*[6] must be an important part of any discussion of pre-1914 unemployment policy, both because of its strengths and its weaknesses. The great strength of Stedman Jones's analysis is the detailed elaboration of the various ways in which unemployment was constructed as a problem in the fifty or so years from the mid-nineteenth century. Central to this construction, he argues, was the stress on casual labour, especially that in London, so that 'when economists, politicians, and pamphleters first talked of "unemployment" they thought of above all the situation in London ... the casual labourers of the Capital'.[7] The centrality of casual labour arose first and foremost from its perceived relation to poverty. In the 1860s and 1870s the problems of the East End were seen through the 'distorting lens' of pauperism and demoralization:

> pauperism, poverty's visible form, was largely an act of will. It had been freely chosen and was therefore sinful. The pauper way of life had been chosen because the negligence and thoughtlessness of the rich had made the state of mendicancy more agreeable than the state of labour. By ensuring through the tightening up of charity and poor law that mendicancy was made less eligible than labour, pauperism, and economic immorality among the London working class, it was assumed, would be gradually eliminated.[8]

In the 1880s, when the word unemployment became widely used, the basis of poverty (not pauperism) was seen as essentially environmental – the degeneration brought about by exposure to the physical and moral pressures of city life. The unemployed were mainly those whose conditions of life made them likely to fall victim to these degenerative influences – which meant mainly the casual labourers. It was recognized that the unemployed artisan existed.[9] He was not, however, important as a problem in his own right, merely as a category to be clearly separated both analytically and administratively from the casual.

The unemployed (the casuals) became a threat in the 1880s (and therefore an object of policy concern) not only because of their propensity to degenerate, and the danger this posed for the classes above them, but also because of their alleged political threat to the existing order, especially if allied to the more respectable but also more politicized 'respectable' part of the working class. This threat received some support from the considerable unrest during the depression of 1886–7, and the role of the small but vocal socialist groups like the Social Democratic Federation.

Finally, Stedman Jones argues, from 1890 the concern with the casual labourer was linked to two particular conceptions. Firstly that casual unemployment and chronic poverty threatened the fitness of the British race to fight imperial wars – threatened 'national efficiency'. Secondly that conception already implied the need to separate the mass of the artisans from contagion by the casuals, by not allowing the former's conditions to deteriorate too sharply in times of trade depression.[10]

Thus, the general argument runs, throughout this period it was the casual labourer who was the focus of the unemployment problem, but that, at the same time, the terms of this problem changed in a complex way. However Stedman Jones' argument of these points is inextricably bound up with a particular conception of ideology, around which the book is structured. This conception is that these various terms within which the problem of the casual labourer was discussed should be seen as a distortion, a misrecognition of the *real* problem.

The real problem, he argues, was the persistence of widespread poverty through the nineteenth century, mainly because of the prevalence of casual labour, itself caused by the decline of heavy industry in the face of coal-based competition from firms in the provinces and the attempts to cut overheads in consumer industries by 'sweating' (rather than the adoption of factory methods). Thus London became dominated by small scale finishing trades which faced seasonal demands for their products to which many employers responded by employing the bulk of their labour force on a seasonal basis. In addition, the very large employing industries of docking and building were also subject to seasonal fluctuations. This seasonal pattern, combined with a general over-supply of labour, provided the major foundations for widespread casual employment which Stedman Jones estimates embraced 10 per cent of London's population by the 1880s, concentrated in the East End.[11]

This real problem provided material support for all the conceptions of casual labour and unemployed noted above, but these in turn distorted understanding of the real problem. *Outcast London* thus works with a real/ideological dichotomy, the ideological (commonly thought through visual metaphors: 'social prism', p.327, 'distorting lens', p.262) as a misrecognition of the real. The central problem of this conception is how the 'real' problem is known. The book does not argue this point, but takes it for granted that certain forms of knowledge are obviously superior to others, a superiority founded ultimately upon epistemological criteria.[12] Only in this way can a complete anti-relativism be justified; some knowledges reveal the truth, others simply obscure it.

Whilst Stedman Jones certainly does not analyse ideology in the functionalist way common in much Marxism (where ideologies simply serve the needs of particular social classes) he is led into implying such functionalism by the real/ideological couple. If ideologies serve to distort the real they thereby obstruct the transformation of that real; ideology is not only a product of the real but serves also to maintain it. From this kind of conception it is only a short step to a crude reductionism. For example, unemployables never existed 'except as a phantom army called up by late Victorian and Edwardian social science to legitimise its practice'.[13]

These are not just abstract arguments, because the organization of the text of *Outcast London* around the real/ideology dichotomy has considerable effects on the specific arguments put forward. For example whilst the conditions of existence of the *ideologies* are spelt out in some detail[14] the conditions of knowledge of the real are never discussed. How the distorted image of the problem is to be corrected is never spelt out, so knowledge of the real becomes an irrational privilege. If one jettisons epistemological criteria then this problem can be avoided; all conceptions of 'problems' can be seen as having particular conditions of existence (and effects) and these can be analysed as such, without reference to whether or not they represent truth. Such a position does not in fact undercut much of the analysis of *Outcast London* because the conditions and effects of particular forms of analysis do not in general depend upon their epistemological status.[15]

The major exception to this is, as one would expect, that analysis which is presented as being of the *real* problem. The effect of privileging a particular kind of analysis of the casual labour problem is that other equally plausible analyses are not seriously dealt with. For example, as Williams points out,[16] Pigou's analysis of the divergence between private and social cost could plausibly be applied to casual labour; by this form of employment employers were able to push the costs of seasonality and other fluctuations onto the employees. Equally plausible would be an analysis like that of Matthews, where the prevalence of casual labour in pre-1914 Britain is ascribed to 'underdevelopment' in the sense of inadequate capital accumulation. 'The unskilled labour that jostled for jobs at the docks, on the building sites and in many other trades was the remnant of the chronic labour surplus associated with incomplete development.'[17]

The point is not being made that Pigou's and Matthews's analyses are 'better' than Stedman Jones in describing the real problem, but that they are just as plausible as what he posits as his analysis of the real problem. Equally if they are superior to those analyses which stressed the role of 'degeneration', 'demoralization', etc. this has to be argued for, not on grounds of epistemology, but in terms of coherence, necessary assumptions, etc.

These relatively extended comments on Stedman Jones have been made not only because of the pertinence of his analysis for the subject of this chapter, but also because of the pertinence for the whole book. This book attempts to evade posing a 'real' problem as opposed to ideological ones for the kinds of reasons just spelt out. This does not mean, it should be stressed, that all analyses are treated as on a par *except* epistemologically. It is still possible, and indeed necessary, to distinguish between different conceptions of problems, their 'internal' character, coherence, etc., and also their conditions of existence and effects. What is not attempted is to wave a magic wand and pronounce on the 'truth' content of these conceptions.

II

The centrality of casual labour as the object of the unemployment

problem in the late nineteenth century is continued in the early
twentieth. Pre-eminently this is so in the discussions of the Royal
Commission on the Poor Laws of 1905–9. Both the Majority and
Minority Reports stress casual labour as the major cause of
pauperism.[18] For the Majority Report chronic underemployment is
'the new problem' and the continuing growth of casual labour is
strongly asserted.[19] As further discussed below, a major point of
advocacy of labour exchanges by Beveridge and others was their
supposed usefulness in combating casuality.[20]

This stress on casual labour as the 'root of all evil' led to some
measures to aid the 'respectable' labourer temporarily unemployed,
measures with the objective of stopping these elements sliding down
the slippery slope into casual labour. Chamberlain's famous Local
Government Board Circular in 1886 encouraged local authorities to
schedule necessary public works, on a non-pauperizing basis, for
artisans temporarily thrown out of work. In similar vein the 1896
Commission on Distress from Want of Employment was in its terms
of reference asked to distinguish between casuals and the cyclically
unemployed. A decade later the Unemployed Workmen Act of 1905
aimed to 'provide work for the respectable and thrifty person who had
in the past been regularly employed, but who was at the time of
making application to the committee temporarily distressed owing to
inability to obtain employment'.[21]

All the evidence given to the 1905 Royal Commission showed the
inability of such schemes to achieve their objectives.[22] Schemes
established for the benefit of artisans were always flooded by casuals,
refusing to respect the divisions so dear to contemporary conceptions
of the unemployment problem. These conceptions were partially
founded upon Booth's survey, with its elaborate breakdown of
London's population into eight classes. The 1905 Act for example had
been deliberately designed for the relief of Booth's elite classes, D and
E – the 'small regular earners' and 'regular standard rate earners'.[23]

Despite the repeated failures of such schemes what is of note is their
continuation right through into the twentieth century. This continuity
reflected the entrenchment of the conception of the casual labourer as
the centre of attention, the fulcrum of concern, as regards the
unemployed. However this continuity of 'concern' was not based on a
continuity of causes. The reasons for this role of the casual and the
consequential debate varied widely over the period.

As noted above in the 1880s the concern with the casual labourer focused on the environmental causes and the degenerative effects of unemployment. Important in this conception was again Booth who assumed 'it was [the residuum's] environment and especially their constant struggle for work, not personal viciousness nor moral frailty which had degraded them'.[24] The residuum's condition was most dangerous because of the potential effects on the classes above.

It is class B that is *de trop*. The competition of B drags down C and D, and that of C and D hangs heavily upon E.

Here in class B we have the crux of the social problem. Every other class can take care of itself, or could do so, if class B were out of the way. These unfortunate people who form a sort of quagmire must be our principal aim.[25]

Such conceptions of the role of the poorest of the casuals (and the drastic remedies suggested by Booth)[26] rose to prominence in the early years of the twentieth century with revelations about the unfitness of army recruits, allegedly demonstrating the degeneration of the British population and the threat this posed to the continuation of the Empire. These fears are most famously expressed in the terms of reference and Report of the Interdepartmental Committee on Physical Deterioration.[27] The Report of this Committee followed Booth in calling for the enforced segregation of the casual poor, and took up his call for labour colonies.

The fears that led up to this Committee's appointment and its own operations were symptomatic of a more widespread movement which has been called the 'Quest for National Efficiency'.[28] This movement embraced a number of diverse strands, the notion of efficiency serving in its ambiguity to structure a set of questions about government, industry and social organization. Nevertheless the clear basis of this movement was 'the revelation of Britain's military incompetence during the Boer War' which led to demands to 'restructure the national life and overhaul the machinery of government, to fit Britain more adequately for the Great Power rivalries of the twentieth century'.[29] The movement was based on a convergence of a wide range of political, social and ideological currents. Pertinent here amongst the latter are both the 'Booth' concern with the casual poor as contaminators of those above, and the growing role of eugenic arguments which attempted to focus attention on the 'excessive' reproduction of the casual poor.[30]

Politically, the concern with national efficiency embraced Fabians,

Tories and the more Imperialist minded sections of the Liberal Party. Perhaps the crucial dividing line between this motley collection and their opponents was the question of the role of the state. For at the centre of the propositions of the 'efficients' were proposals to reform the state machine. This involved both changes in the workings of Cabinet and Parliament, and administrative reform.[31]

This concern to extend and rationalize the state machine raises two important general points in relation to discussion of policy. Firstly the diversity of political elements supporting such proposals is an important corrective to organizing discussion of social policy around a historical political divide between Left and Right which is coterminous with 'state intervention' versus 'laissez-faire' (see further below). Such an identification is of course one which is not just retrospective – Booth for example identified the Poor Laws with socialism, and his critics attacked his calls for extensions of the Poor Laws on that ground.[32] Opposition to 'collectivism', mainly within the Liberal Party, was a major reason why only small elements of the 'efficient's' programme was passed into legislation during the Liberal government of 1905–14; despite a consensus amongst experts and social reformers.[33]

Secondly, the concern with administrative means underlines the particular character of unemployment policy at this time. Unemployment was a 'social' problem, a problem to be solved by social-administrative means – the reform of the poor laws, the creation of new state agencies like labour exchanges and social insurance. At one level these means were classically laissez-faire – they did not involve any direct intervention into the economy as constituted by classical political economy – the production and distribution of wealth. They can be seen as simply measures to rationalize and extend that framework of state action within which market forces can operate and which ideologues of laissez-faire have always supported. In the case of unemployment such a conception is best seen in the work of Beveridge,[34] the major proponent of labour exchanges. But Beveridge was more important than simply a proponent of the extension of orthodox conceptions of state action in the labour market. His 'extension' involved a new framework which in turn was a major part in the reorganization of the whole terrain on which unemployment as a policy problem came to be discussed.

III

In many ways Beveridge's book can be readily assimilated to the kinds of concern predominant in discussions of unemployment from the 1880s. The book's central concern is with casuality. 'The first object of the organisation of the labour market is to make possible a policy of "decasualisation".'[35] It sees the problem as essentially an administrative one – to create new agencies of social administration.. And the book is in step with Booth and others in calling for harsh measures for those beyond redemption, 'means for separating from society those who are clearly unfit to belong thereto – something corresponding to the penal colonies in Belgium and Switzerland. This is for the "unemployable" who perhaps cannot be made good again.'[36]

Despite these similarities Beveridge's book is not just a continuation of an established refrain. In particular the concern with casual labour is constructed in an entirely new way. The prevalence of this kind of employment is seen as a particularly clear example of a general failing of the labour market, 'the maladjustment between the supply of and the demand for labour'.[37] This maladjustment is general, extending to the most skilled trades, and it is this which can be tackled and solved by policy. Other reasons for unemployment exist – seasonal, frictional and cyclical – but these 'spring from one or more of the fundamental facts of modern life. They probably cannot be eliminated without an entire reconstruction of the industrial order.' The only aim in relation to these causes can be palliation.

Thus, for Beveridge, unemployment is a diverse problem, but above all an *economic* one. 'Economic' here has a precise meaning – the relation between supply and demand (for labour). It is these forces which generate unemployment. Today such a conception might be thought a banality, but then it broke new ground. For example whilst classical political economy did of course conceive of the labour market as operating in the same way as other markets, that market had never been investigated seriously as a mechanism. Whilst orthodox economists accepted the role of wage movements in regulating employment, they generally treated unemployment as a branch of the theory of short-term monetary disorder.[38] By contrast Beveridge's whole emphasis was on the mechanism of the labour market, and how it could be made to work effectively.

Whilst, as already noted, Beveridge was far from adopting a 'soft' attitude to the unemployed, the conception of the causes of unemployment as essentially economic necessarily broke up the ground upon which previous discussion of unemployment had been based. Individual 'character' was still relevant to unemployment but not as first cause. Character either acted as a selection mechanism determining who would be subject to economic forces — so that the total number unemployed was not determined by character — or character deteriorated because of unemployment and so was not the initial problem.[39]

In this way Beveridge established a new terrain for the discussion of unemployment. Of course concern with individual character in relation to unemployment does not disappear overnight. Its continuation is reflected in discussions of pauperism and demoralization in the mass unemployment of the 1920s.[40] But from Beveridge onwards the focus of the unemployment 'problem' shifts towards non-personal forces, towards the operations of economic forces.

But few terms could be more ambiguous than 'economic forces'. This ambiguity is registered by Harris.

> although unemployment was increasingly recognised as an 'economic' question, the consideration of practical remedies involved few of the theoretical economic questions that characterised the debate on unemployment after the First World War. The majority of writers on the subject before 1914 did not identify unemployment with deflation, high interest rates, adherence to the gold standard or maintenance of the value of the pound ... Throughout this period the history of unemployment policy at all levels ... is therefore primarily concerned with problems of social administration.[41]

Clearly the problem with this argument is that the ambiguities of 'economic' are not made explicit. 'Economic' before the First World War was not of course the 'economic' of Keynesian economics but then there is no good reasoin to adopt the latter as the standard by which to judge all other analyses. Beveridge's 'economic' was obviously perfectly compatible with 'social-administrative' measures precisely because the problem was one of the market mechanism and not of the 'economy as a whole' — consumption, investment, government budgetary policy — in Keynesian terms.

This difference between Beveridge's and Keynes's 'economy' is not only important in order to highlight the ambiguities of that word. It also serves to underline the fatuity of discussing policies on unemployment in terms of laissez-faire versus state intervention. On this basis both Beveridge and Keynes would be conceived as advocates of 'state intervention', but the character of those interventions, and the conceptions on which their advocacy was based could hardly differ more.[42]

To summarize: despite the clear links between Beveridge's kind of analysis and others in play after the 1880s, his work played a crucial part in placing unemployment policy on a different basis, though other elements were of course important (see Chapter 4). This basis was not that of modern macroeconomic discussions. Its conception of economic was a precise and different one. But by destroying much of the basis for discussion of unemployment in relation to individual character he opened a space for later constructions of unemployment as an 'economic' problem in a wide range of senses of that word.

A parallel argument could be applied to one of the social-administrative reforms worked for by Beveridge, social insurance against unemployment. This stemmed from typical late nineteenth-century concerns, aid to the temporarily unemployed artisan, and a means of penalizing the casual worker and his employer.[43] But its consequences were wholly unplanned; after 1918 it also played a significant part in the construction of unemployment as an 'economic' problem (see Chapter 4).

IV

The way in which unemployment as a problem was constructed as a problem before World War One could be read as simply an example of pre-Keynesian ignorance.[44] The problems with this kind of approach are manifest. It establishes a standard of judgement which proves less permanent than might be hoped – economics has its 'counter-revolutions' as well as its 'revolutions'. Equally it poses the same issues as are raised by the notion of the 'real' problem discussed above. Agents and agencies of the pre-Keynesian period, ignorant of their own 'ignorance', constructed problems and policies which had effects wholly independently of that ignorance, and which can be understood without any necessary reference to any later analysis which posed the problem in a different way. For these reasons policy and the conceptions which inform it are best understood not as a groping towards a light at the end of the tunnel, for what is conceived of as the tunnel and what as the light is constantly being recast and reorganized.

Britain and the gold standard 1880–1914

To discuss the pre-1914 gold standard in a book about problems of British economic policy is something of a paradox. For the striking feature of the gold standard in this period was that, in one important sense, it was not a 'problem'. No institutions or social forces offered a serious challenge to British adherence to the standard. But this in itself is a problem in another sense; why was this central part of the British economic arrangements taken so much for granted? How did the gold standard become regarded as almost a natural phenomenon? What were the implications for economic policy? These are the main questions which are at issue in this chapter.

Concentration on these questions means that this chapter does not generally attempt to deal with the same questions as the enormous existing literature on the gold standard. The starting point here is however linked to one major theme of that literature – its stress on the non-automatic nature of that standard. The conception of the gold standard as an automatic one was classically encapsulated in the Cunliffe Report of 1918. This asserted that 'Before the war the country possessed a complete and effective gold standard. The provisions of the Bank Act, 1844, operated automatically to correct unfavourable exchanges and to check undue expansions of credit.'[1] The conception of an automatic, mechanistic standard was attacked as long ago as 1936 by Sayers,[2] who attempted to show the conditions, especially the immediate institutional financial conditions, which made the policy of adherence to the gold standard possible.

In this chapter the starting point is this conception of a nonautomatic standard. To argue that the standard was not 'automatic' is to argue that its operations were not independent of the practices of the institution on which it rested. So one must, as Sayers does, discuss these immediate institutional practices. But discussion of the practices opens up questions about the support of these practices – how are they to be understood, on what preconditions did they in turn rest? No exhaustive answer can be given to these questions, and my aim has been to discuss those preconditions which are necessary to understand the particularities of the pre-1914 standard, and conversely those which feed into understanding the fate of the gold standard after the First World War (see below Chapter 6). Secondly I want to discuss the relation of these conditions to economic policy. Whilst adherence to the gold standard in the late nineteenth century does appear an almost 'natural' phenomenon, it was of course both the effect of policy decisions and in turn had effects on policy.

I

It is a commonplace of modern discussions of the gold standard to at least gesture towards the wider, non-financial conditions of the world economy, and Britain's dominance within it, which underlay the operations of the standard. While this is more helpful than the Cunliffe approach, in which the gold standard appears as a kind of supra-historical mechanism with virtually no conditions of existence, it also has dangers. Particularly, it commonly leads to a kind of reductionism in which the existence of the gold standard is seen simply as an effect of developments in the real[3] economy. Thus Hobsbawm[4] writes, 'the stability of the British currency rested on the international hegemony of the British economy, and when it ceased, no amount of Bank Rate manipulation did much good'. Such reductionism short-circuits most of the interesting problems. The conditions of survival of the gold standard are lost to view in that most oft repeated of modern morality tales, the decline of the British economy.

One way into such problems is to ask the question, why was Britain on the gold standard at all? De Cecco[5] has shown the conditions under which a variety of countries came on to the gold standard in the late nineteenth century, but even he takes at least Britain's initial adherence for granted. This lack of consideration arises in part from two related reasons. Whilst in many countries in the late nineteenth century the question of adherence to the gold standard was an important public issue, what dispute there was in Britain on this subject was extremely muted and never amounted to a serious threat to Britain's adherence. Secondly, British adherence to the gold standard was uniquely long standing, whilst most other countries only came on the gold standard after 1870.

To take the latter point first. Britain was de facto on the gold standard, that is the pound was convertible into a fixed amount of gold, from the early eighteenth century.[6] The greatest arguments over this adherence came later, however, during and after the period when the gold standard was suspended in 1797 and (completely) restored in 1821.

One of the many ingredients in disputes at this time, and something which is a recurrent feature of the history of the gold standard, is the position and powers of the Bank of England. At the end of the Napoleonic Wars one of the most powerful arguments used in favour of the resumption of specie payments was hostility to the Bank of England which was seen as having waxed fat in the restriction period, and to be arrogating itself unconstitutional powers in opposing the resumption of gold payments.[7] This particular case of opposition to the powers of one institution (albeit a private one) provided a support for generalized opposition to discretionary monetary management which has been a concomitant to support for the gold standard up until the present day.[8] In the conditions of early nineteenth-century Britain, opposition to discretionary monetary management had a different political hue than is usually the case today. Working-class spokesmen opposed such management because it would mean control by either an aristrocacy-dominated government or a Bank run by a 'company of traders'.[9]

One other ramification of these arguments is of note. Fetter[10] locates a major support of Say's Law in these political disputes over monetary policy, rather than (as more usual) discussing the Law in only theoretical terms. He points out that the clear implication of Say's Law was that government intervention in relation to unemployment was unnecessary because the economy was self-stabilizing at a full employment level. This provided a supporting contention for working-class spokesmen opposed to discretionary monetary management. (This use of Say's Law was again of course different in political hue from its use in twentieth-century arguments about unemployment, where the extension of state intervention is generally the prerogative of the Left.)

Later the arguments over the institutional effects of the gold standard took different forms. Cunliffe, for example, linked the restoration of the gold standard to the restoration of the Bank of

England's power over the note issue (para. 47). The Treasury's issuing of notes was seen as both directly instrumental in the inflation leading to the breakdown of the gold standard, and also 'improper' as putting the issuing of currency in the hands of the executive rather than the Bank. But this does not detract from the general point that the question of adherence to the gold standard has always been in part a question of the distribution of power between institutions.

Equally recurrent has been the question of the distributional effects of adherence to the gold standard. There was widespread acceptance in the post-Napoleonic period that restoration meant deflation as the money supply contracted. The effects of such deflation were seen largely in relation to distribution, rather than total employment (though this was raised by a minority).[11] However, strikingly, no strong political movement against these deflationary consequences emerged. The argument that deflation would hit the purses of the landed gentry was put, but received little support.[12] Most opposition to the restoration was conservative in nature, radicals for the most part, and for the reasons already mentioned, being in favour of the restoration.

At the time of these disputes, practically no other country was on the gold standard, most countries coming on to the standard much later than Britain – in 1870 for example the only other country on was Portugal.[13] But once on the standard most other countries had widespread disputes about such adherence in a way absent in *late* nineteenth-century Britain. A major reason for these disputes in other countries was the coincidence after 1873 of falling gold prices for commodities and the widespread demonetarization of silver. Debtors in such countries linked the increasing real burden of their debts (i.e. falling prices) with the restrictions on the money supply caused by the coming of the mono-metallic gold standard, and campaigned for the reversion to a silver or bi-metallic standard which would expect the monetary base. Most famous is the struggle in the United States, where for over twenty years the question of the standard was a major political dispute gaining particularly widespread agrarian support. The dispute was not finally ended until after the defeat of the silver candidate, Bryan, in the 1896 Presidential elections.

More successful than the American inflationists were the Argentinian landowners, often mortgate debtors, who were the major component of the Argentinian ruling class. They were able to take Argentina off the gold standard in 1884 only a year after formally rejoining. As well as their debtor position these dominant elements in Argentina were motivated by their desire to prevent the gold standard restricting their ability to finance government expenditure by currency issue rather than taxation of their own incomes.[14] Argentina's position was also conditioned by the particular position of the banks, which unlike the position in many British Empire countries, were not to any great extent overseas banks providing internal credit facilities and where foreign exchange reserves were not held by such banks. So the 'technical' problem of controlling the note issue compounded the political opposition to any such policy.

By contrast it is interesting to ask why such arguments were so muted in Britain. At no time in the late nineteenth century could it be said that Britain's adherence to the gold standard was open to serious doubt.[15] There was considerable official and academic discussion of the desirability of bi-metallism, and an official committee[16] set up to consider the issue was equally divided on whether Britain should go over to a bi-metallic system. By contrast with what was happening and being said in other countries a striking aspect of the Commission's Report is the tiny part played in it by discussion of income distribution. Whilst both the opposing groups on the Commission accepted that the depreciation of silver was having adverse effects on Britain, these adverse effects were mainly seen as being on trade between gold and silver countries (especially Britain and India); on investment by gold in silver countries (especially again Britain and India); and the problem of the remittance of funds from India to London. Thus the great stress was on international problems, especially those in relation to India which happened to be both economically Britain's most important colony and the world's most important silver user.

The general deflation in England is put down to causes other than monetary by the opponents of bi-metallism (e.g. Part II, para. 88) and to largely monetary causes by the supporters (Part III, para. 10). But even the latter group do not argue that the main effect of the deflation was a redistributive one, suggesting instead (on the basis of very slim evidence, Part III, para. 19) that the fall in prices was causing unemployment and a fall in money wages.

What then needs to be explained is the absence in Britain of any politically powerful 'inflationist' movement based on a debtor class. The general reasons for this may not be difficult to see. The agricultural sector in Britain, however measured, was much smaller than in any other major country. In 1871 only 14 per cent of the British labour force was in agriculture, compared with over 50 per cent in the United States.[17] British agriculture was by this time, of course, thoroughly capitalist. The bulk of the agricultural population were wage labourers who gained from falling prices. Tenant farmers were commonly in a good enough bargaining position to reduce their rents. The effects of generally falling agricultural prices (particularly severe in Britain because of the absence of protection) seem therefore to have been borne mainly by the landlords, many of whom had long since spread their interests into mining, urban property and industry.[18]

So whilst landlords, particularly in the South Eastern parts of England, *did* complain vociferously about falling prices and agricultural depression, and two Royal Commissions heard their complaints,[19] the complaints did not crystallize into a political movement as in the USA. Compared with that country, not enough people were being 'crucified on a cross of gold' – the total agricultural population was too small, and the peasant ('family farm') organization almost entirely absent. The British rural population was not characteristically a debtor group.

This line of argument may be seen as inconsistent, falling within the 'representation of interests' theme criticized in the Introduction. However the point which was stressed in the Introduction was the problem of *representation*–and its problematic nature in the analysis of policy making. The problems of 'representation of interest' do not mean that the notion of interest groups has to be totally discarded. Interests in the sense of individuals or groups of agents which calculate certain objectives for themselves seem an inescapable, if limited, component of social analysis. What has to be discarded is firstly the 'obviousness' which is commonly ascribed to these calculated objectives, whereas stress on their *calculation* means that what any agents may conceive of as in their interest is highly problematic. Secondly, it is not the postulation of interests but the reduction of policy to the representation of these interests which is problematic for the analysis of policy.

In the present chapter the point is not that if the gold standard had 'hurt' the interests of a large part of the population this would automatically have led to the representation of this injury in the form of pressures for the end of the standard. Both the above general points apply here. The argument that the gold standard, by causing deflation, 'hurts' the populace is precisely an *argument*, it is not an unchallengeable effect of the real world. Therefore if there had been a correlation between the adherence to gold and widespread falling living standards this might have provided a purchase not only for those advocating leaving gold but for a whole range of other positions, e.g. debt renunciation, or the issue of unbacked paper money.

Secondly, even if the populace had perceived an injury as inflicted by adherence to gold, the *means* by which they attempted to redress that hurt would have its own particular effects. For example, working through parliamentary channels would have different conditions and implications from attempts via revolutionary action.

To sum up, what is being argued here is that, in the absence of such a correlation between widespread falling living standards and adherence to gold, the space for a whole range of arguments was not available, including that of opposition to that adherence. Of course, given absence of this 'space' the question of which particular argument and which means of representation does not even arise.

This absence of an effective challenge to the gold standard by inflationists was paralleled by the absence of any effective challenge to anyone opposed to the general subordination of national economic policy to international economic events. This is not surprising perhaps, but worthy of remark. It was something common to most other gold standard countries. No political force had yet appeared to challenge the domination of monetary policy by international considerations. This can be understood at a number of levels. Partly of course the whole conception of a national economy to be managed did not exist at this time, and such a conception was indeed partly predicated on the absence of a gold standard (see below, Chapter 8). Secondly, such subordination was less likely to be challenged because of the effects of falling prices in the late nineteenth century. In a country like Britain where most of the population were wage earners, not peasants or farmers, the fall in prices produced a sharp rise in real wages. 'Between 1880 and 1900, for the industrial worker who stayed in the same occupation, money wage rates increased on the average by 15 to 20 per cent, while retail prices fell by about 15 per cent.'[20] The situation was *not* like the 1920s when a strong working-class movement faced the prospect of falling living standards as a consequence of rejoining the gold standard at the $4.86 parity.

The nascent working-class movement in Britain therefore had no reason to make the gold standard a contentious issue. And unlike Argentina, the most politically powerful class was not the landowners but the industrial and financial capitalists. If the three decades prior to the First World War were the heyday of the gold standard, they were also the heyday of the British investor abroad: the two things were intimately linked.

The extent of British long-term capital exports relative to National Income in this period was unprecedented and has nowhere near been exceeded since. Lindert[21] points out that between a quarter and a third of British wealth was at this time held abroad, and that this was relatively much greater than the sums lent abroad by the most important international creditor since the Second World War, the United States. Equally unprecedented was the scale of British liquid assets – London was a uniquely attractive centre in which to invest short-term funds.

These capital movements are central to the pre-1914 gold standard. Adherence to the standard meant that a central object of policy was a *stable* exchange rate. A stable exchange rate was central because without it the movement of international capital would have been imperilled. So under a gold standard regime the *level* of the exchange rate is not a policy issue. Countries may be forced off gold, they *do not* devalue. The level of the exchange is mostly pertinent to the trade balance and in nineteenth-century England the trade balance was not an object of policy.

Of course there were enormous arguments in the late nineteenth century about Britain's foreign trade and the 'need' for protection. But these were not arguments in modern terms about the need to correct an inverse balance of trade. Indeed as Clapham[22] points out the Protectionist/Free Trader arguments were often couched directly in terms of the effects of trade on Britain's gold reserves. The protectionists argued that the free market meant Britain paid her adverse balance in sovereigns, the free traders retorting that on the contrary free trade always brought in the necessary gold.

The central object of international economic policy was precisely these gold reserves. As Sayers[23] notes, changes in Bank Rate have nothing to do with 'price levels, the supply of money, the state of credit, employment or even speculation. A rise is directed simply at securing gold.' The conception of a policy towards the 'balance of payments', and indeed that notion itself, had not yet been born. The modern notion of the balance of payments is probably best understood as a corollary of the notion of national economy – which was absent at this time. (The lack of the concept was also the lack of data – balance of payments figures for this period being a retrospective creation.)[24]

Whilst the modern conception of the balance of payments and trade was absent in the nineteenth century, and therefore absent as a policy objective, the pattern of trade and payments was central to the operation of the gold standard. The policy of free trade pursued by Britain meant a gradual deterioration of Britain's visible trade balance in the nineteenth century. The visible deficit rose from around £60m per annum in the 1860s to average over £140m per annum in the 1890s.[25] Under these conditions the British payments position became effectively reliant on an invisible surplus to offset this deficit and provide the finance for capital exports. Britain's ability to generate this invisible surplus was dependent on a number of other features of the British economy.

First it was linked to Britain's share in world trade, especially her role as the largest export market by far. In 1872–3 for example Britain still bought more than 25 per cent of all the exports (f.o.b.) of other countries and in *absolute* terms the amount was still expanding fast. This scale of imports was both a 'problem' but also part of the solution by providing a substantial basis for invisible earnings.[26] Given Britain's dominance of world shipping, invisible earnings on shipping account grew rapidly to around the £100m per annum mark by the eve of the First World War. The provision of shipping to the world's traders was in turn linked to the provision of insurance services to these traders. The other main source of invisible earnings (ignoring the cumulative returns on foreign long-term investment) was by the granting of short-term credits by the London money market, especially in the form of international bills of exchange. Whilst the contribution of this latter to the balance of payments has been disputed (see below, Section II) its contribution to making London the world's chief money market is open to no doubt. As discussed below, the movement of funds in and out of London created a major condition for the effectiveness of the British Bank Rate in attracting and repelling funds in and out of London.

No one, of course, planned the late nineteenth-century international economy, nor Britain's place in it. Yet the two policies of adherence to the gold standard and free trade were in a mutually supporting position. Free trade meant for Britain a substantial and worsening visible trade position. The ability to sustain this rested to a large extent on Britain's capacity to attract foreign funds, in part because of the stability imparted by the gold standard. Conversely, adherence to gold was in part dependent on free trade, because this generated an enormous British trade which made sterling both a readily available and attractive currency to hold. This symbiotic relation between free gold and free trade was highly specific to Britain in this period. Other countries at the same time, and of course Britain in an earlier period, combined adherence to gold with protection in trade. It is nicely appropriate that the crucial events leading to the end of the gold standard should be in 1931, coinciding with the decisive blows to free trade in Britain.

II

The general points above outline some of the conditions which made both plausible and possible the sustaining of the gold standard until the First World War. However to leave the question there would be to make the operation of the gold standard largely innocent of institutional practices. Without consideration of these practices the reductionist accounts of the gold standard and its conditions of existence appear correct, as the gold standard's survival hinged simply on the existence of Britain's domination of the world economy and other such generalities.

Of the specific institutions sustaining the gold standard, the Bank of England was of course central. The Bank remained both in law and in practice a private institution throughout the nineteenth century. Its privileged position as the monopoly note issuer and holder of the country's gold reserves arose not from any clear theory of central banking, but from a series of conjunctures, a series of 'political motives and historical accidents'.[27]

Founded initially to circumvent the monarchy's financial problems following Charles I's reneging on his debts, it had been greatly aided by the circumstances of the Napoleonic wars in which it had expanded its credit to the government in return for being effectively promised to be bailed out of any crisis. The notes of the Bank were formally made legal tender in 1812, and an Act of 1826 put restrictions on other banks' note-issuing powers. By the Bank Charter Act of 1844 the Bank of England became the 'tool' for regulating the money supply through its control of the note issue. Other banks were willing to cede this monopoly position to the Bank because by mid-century the rise of cheques meant that the note issue was becoming less important in the total monetary circulation.

Theoretical arguments might continue to be put forward for the superiority of multiple reserve, 'free banking', systems – and Bagehot in *Lombard Street*[28] advanced such arguments. But no effective opposition to the Bank of England's monopoly of the note issue existed in late nineteenth-century England and Wales (Scotland retained a separate system, and is commonly used as an example of a successful multiple issue system).[29] On this monopoly of the note issue was founded the monopoly of the gold reserves – though this latter was later challenged (see below).

Perhaps it should be stressed more than is usual that the powerful position of the Bank of England over such a long stretch of time appears in restrospect something to be explained rather than just taken for granted. Viner points to this longevity and puts it down largely to the 'conservatism of its management and to the moderation, at least since 1689, of British politics'.[30] More particularly we have seen how the powers of the Bank were challenged at the end of the Napoleonic wars and how adherence to the gold standard was seen as restricting such powers.

The Bank's powers were also challenged by Gladstone in mid-century. An important part of his policy of balanced or surplus budgets was not so much an 'ideological' obsession as a weapon to strengthen the Treasury against the Bank. He felt that the state was in a 'false' position in relation to the Bank and the City. Budget surpluses meant that 'a Chancellor now never had to beg'.[31] The Post Office Savings Bank was set up for similar reasons. Overall, however, once the Bank had achieved a monopoly position over the note issue it was always likely to be protected by the government, especially when, despite Gladstone's efforts, government borrowing increased and the Bank played its role as manager of the National Debt.

The private legal status of the Bank in the nineteenth century should not be forgotten. This status implied that a major plank of British economic policy, adherence to the gold standard, was regulated by a non-public body, and a body whose deliberations were so closed that the provisions of the 1911 Official Secrets Act appear a charter for open government in comparison. This private legal status of the Bank was not offset by detailed government regulation. Indeed, as Sayers notes, 'The Bank was singularly free of all legislative restriction of its operations'.[32]

One particular practice linked to this unregulated private status was the Bank's desire to maintain the level of dividend payments to shareholders. This was one of the reasons why Britain's gold reserves were so small – gold was not an income-earning asset for the Bank. This parsimony with the reserves in turn meant even a small outflow of gold necessitated a response to the Bank, so that a feature of the Bank of England's policies was the frequent changes in Bank Rate. Thus traders on occasion made unfavourable comparisons between the stability of the Bank of France discount rate and the fluctuations in Bank Rate.[33]

Small reserves were only sustainable at all because of the effectiveness of manipulation of Bank Rate in stemming outflows or encouraging inflows of gold into London. London's domination of the international money market was the general condition for this as suggested above. However the rate was not uniformly effective throughout this period. Funds were not attracted into London by the Bank Rate as such but by the market rate in London. Bank Rate would therefore regulate gold flows only if it first regulated market rates. That this would be so was by no means unproblematic.

In the period 1858-78 the Bank Rate followed the market rate most of the time rather than controlling and the Bank was able to make its rate effective in the market only rarely. Gladstone's policy of cutting the Bank's income from government was one part of the reason for this, because it meant the Bank chased business rather than holding up the Bank Rate.[34] In addition the main way the Bank in this period could affect the market rate, open market operations, was used infrequently as the Bank had to bear the interest cost of the funds it took out of the market.

After 1878 the Bank's control increased. Having seen its share of discount business dwindle the Bank decided to make the discount rate charged to its own customers independent of Bank Rate. This meant Bank Rate could be used in a new way – as a penal rate. Funds would thereby always be available to the discount houses – but at a high rate of interest. In consequence the discount houses could work on low cash margins and resort to the Bank in times of trouble. In turn this meant that the Bank Rate became important to the houses, and so became important to the whole money market, and led market rates rather than following. As the discount market was by this time largely an international market, the Bank Rate became most important for its effects on international gold flows. This was especially so after 1890 when cash flows from the country banks to the Bank more or less disappeared following the Baring Crisis.[35]

The increasing effectiveness of Bank Rate meant that its fluctuations were more likely to be criticized. In the 1890s[36] sensitivity to such criticisms and doubts about the attractive power of a high Bank Rate led to more use of the gold 'devices', i.e. direct operations in the gold market such as offering above the official price for bullion, or giving interest-free loans to gold importers. However this point should not be stressed too much, 'this tenderness for home trade was subordinate to the primary object of protecting the gold reserve'.[37] Particularly after the turn of the century with Bank Rate seemingly more effective in attracting gold the use of the 'devices' more or less ceased.

As is apparent from the above discussion, the effectiveness of the Bank of England in controlling the gold reserve was based in turn on the role of two other institutions in particular – the discount market and the gold market.

The rise to prominence of the international bill in the London financial market was the effect of two sets of conditions. The first of these sets was that which led to the disappearance of the inland Bill of Exchange. This disappearance resulted from general economic changes along with a change in the institutional context. The former was the improvement of transport, in particular the extension of the rail network, which led to fewer calls for extended credit terms to finance internal trade. The latter and perhaps the more significant change was the amalgamation of the banks which meant that the redistribution of credit between different geographical centres was largely *within* particular institutions. This meant that the bill of exchange, used for transfers *between* institutions, was no longer required by traders. In addition, the cheque developed as a more flexible instrument than the bill. This process was added to by the decreased willingness of country banks to rediscount after the financial crisis of 1857.[38]

The rise of the international bill was partly the effect of free trade and the subsequent expansion of British trade in particular and world trade in general.[39] In the conditions of the late-nineteenth century, with London a willing lender and the pound a pre-eminently stable currency, the bill provided an ideal form of credit for international trade.

More specifically the Franco-Prussian War prevented France, Britain's main competitor in the money market, from actively challenging London's role. (In addition, the French indemnity to the

Reich was transformed by Germany into large floating balances in London.) Other rival centres were also undermined: for example New York by the dollar being 'buried under Greenbacks' in 1865–6; Germany by its relatively late arrival on the gold standard (1873).

Upon the centrality of the international bill of exchange was founded London's dominant role in short-term lending and borrowing. The crucial factor for the operation of the gold standard was not Britain's creditor or debtor position. Despite the claims of the Macmillan Report[40] it is not clear that Britain before the First World War was a net creditor on short-term account. But as Ford points out, this was not the crucial point: as long as an increased Bank Rate was effective in keeping balances in London, a sufficient condition for the gold standard to work was provided.[41]

For centres without this volume of short-term funds constantly coming and going, the effects of discount rate changes could be 'perverse', i.e. a higher rate being taken to imply instability, leading to capital flight. This peculiar position of Britain was enhanced by the stability of the pound on the gold standard. As Lindert[42] has pointed out, it is somewhat paradoxical that the greater the (expected) stability of the gold exchange rate, the greater the willingness to hold foreign balances rather than gold in the national reserves. London was the main recipient of such balances globally, though in Europe (including Russia) the holding of francs and marks was more popular than holding sterling.[43] This obviously implies that holding sterling was particularly attractive to countries in non-European areas, especially Africa, Asia and Australia.

London's role as the favoured site for reserves of both gold and sterling was partly the effect of the Empire. India's sterling and gold reserves in December 1912 are shown in Table 2.1. In so far as these reserves were held in London they provided 'a large *masse de manoeuvre* which British monetary authorities could use to supplement their own reserves and to keep London the centre of the international monetary system'.[44] A similar effect was produced by the reserves of the Straits Settlements, the conversion funds of South American Republics and so on.[45] Obviously these latter countries, not part of the Empire, were not coerced into holding reserves in London – such a policy made good financial sense. However, in the crucial case of India, the holding of reserves in London was seen by Nationalists very much as a sign of subordination to London policy makers and financiers. Paradoxically perhaps, the fact of India's political subservience to London may have made the holding of reserves in London less palatable than it might have been if, as in South America, (formal) political independence had been obtained.[46]

Table 2.1 India's gold and sterling reserves, December 1912.

	£
Gold	
Currency Reserve in India	17,500,000
Currency Reserve in London	7,250,000
Gold Standard Reserve in London	250,000
Money at Short Notice	
Gold Standard Reserve in London	1,000,000
Cash Balances in London	7,500,000
Sterling Securities	
Currency Reserves	2,500,000
Gold Standard Reserve	16,000,000
Total	52,000,000

Source: J.M. Keynes, *Indian Currency and Finance*, 1913 (*Collected Writings* I 1971), p.131.

Whilst the immense flows of long-term capital from Britain before 1914 were rarely directed by overt political motives (unlike, for example, French investment in Russia), political reasons were quite important for short-term capital flows. Especially important after 1900 was the holding of Japanese balances in London, a 'cement' to the two countries' political alliance.[47]

London was not only the major focus of flows of short-term funds before 1913 but also the site of the world's most important gold market. In the late nineteenth century this was aided by the fact that the main source of gold was in an Empire country – South Africa. Almost all the gold sold abroad from the Witwatersrand mines passed through London, even if relatively small amounts found their final sale there. This flow meant that gold was always available in London if required. So the trade in gold became one more support for London's position. As early as the 1850s, as Clapham notes,[48] 'In the financial journalism of the day it is remarkable how prominent are the names of ships and the figures of the gold that they carry'.

III

The concept of a 'heyday' for the gold standard before 1914 clearly implies that the First World War was central to the breakdown of that standard. Thus the sharp deterioration in Britain's international economic position as a result of the war (the loss of export markets, the liquidation of foreign assets, the rise of the USA as a creditor country, etc.) was closely tied to the demise of gold. This conception has however been challenged by de Cecco[49] who argues that the system was already crisis-laden long before 1914.

De Cecco's argument falls into two parts. First he suggests that parallel with the relative decline of Britain's industrial position from *c*. 1890 went a decline in her position as a financial centre, with the development of Paris, Berlin and New York in this role. However, as he himself makes clear, this simple parallel does not really hold up. In the crucial short-term money markets (and also in the area of long-term lending) London retained its predominance. In the central business of accepting and discounting foreign trade bills none of the other centres 'managed to become serious rivals to London by 1914'.[50]

In the second part of his analysis de Cecco moves away from this rather reductionist approach and considers the specific conditions changing the operations of the gold standard especially in the years from the Boer War to 1914. Here his argument is more convincing. In particular, he cites the well-known phenomenon of increasing holdings of foreign exchange reserves before 1913, not, as Keynes did,[51] as a sign of a favourable development in the international monetary system, but as a sign of its crisis. De Cecco suggests that increased holdings of foreign exchange were not so much a sign of increasing faith in the stability of the 'key currencies' (particularly sterling) but as a sign of a growing unwillingness to lose gold reserves, and therefore the use of foreign exchange reserves to protect them. This accumulation of gold largely reflected the growing threat of war, and therefore a process of 'monetary rearmament'.[52]

For London this process, though partially offset by 'political deposits' in London, meant that gold became less easy to come by, especially in time of crisis, as can be illustrated by reference to the events of 1907. In that year a financial crisis in the USA rapidly reduced the London gold stock from £38m to £31m.[53] In response to this Bank Rate was raised to 7 per cent – a level it had not reached since 1873. Gold flowed in. Partly this was the effect of pressure on

the Bank of France which bought short sterling bills as an alternative
to having to raise its own discount rate. De Cecco argues, however,
that the crucial event which made Bank Rate effective was the
willingness of the USA to bear the burden of readjustment by
drastically decreasing imports and increasing exports.[54]

What this episode points up, once again, is the highly specific
circumstances which made possible the survival of the pre-1914 gold
standard. Even if we fully accept de Cecco's version of the 1907
events this does not necessarily mean we have to accept his conception of a 'general crisis' of the world monetary system, even less do
we have to accept the crisis as simply a parallel of the decline of London's dominance. As even de Cecco's account makes clear, despite decades of Britain's 'relative decline' Bank Rate *was* still effective in
increasing the Bank of England's gold reserve in 1907. And there is
no clear reason why the particular reasons for this effectiveness in
1907 are any more signs of a 'general crisis' than the different particular
reasons for its effectiveness at earlier points.

This last argument is not aimed at denying the problems of the
international gold standard before 1914. De Cecco highlights some
problems previously given little emphasis – especially the large and
regular gold flows to the USA. However what is at stake here is not
his detailed arguments, but the general conception of a simple
determinism of the financial system by the 'underlying' economy.
This chapter has aimed to show, amongst other things, the limitations
of such a conception.

IV

Overall the arguments of this chapter may be summarized as follows.
Britain's adherence to the gold standard, like other 'laissez-faire'
institutions (for example free trade, the poor law), was not the absence
of a policy but a particular kind of state policy. In the case of the gold
standard this meant a policy of creating and maintaining a private
institution (the Bank of England) as a monopoly holder of gold
reserves and, progressively, a monopoly note issuer. In the conditions
of this period that meant that it was virtually the controller of national
monetary policy. Whilst adherence to gold was a state policy, it was
not a 'problem' in the sense of a contested area where state agencies
had to fight the objectives or means of attaining objectives proposed
by other agencies, or constantly to struggle to realize its own aims.

The conditions for this have, for analytical purposes, been separated into two – the reasons for absence of an anti-gold-standard movement, and the conditions which made Britain's adherence to the standard relatively easy to sustain.

The 'solidity' of Britain's adherence to the gold standard had implications for other problems of economic policy. It meant the almost total *absence* of a problem of a national monetary policy, because adherence to gold implied the subordination of domestic monetary policy to international flows of gold. (A point taken up in Chapters 6 and 8.) Adherence to gold also had effects on the 'problem' of free trade because, together, the two defined Britain's relation to the world economy. This point is taken up in the next chapter.

— 3 —

Trade and Empire before 1914

Arguments over economic policy are always in part arguments over differing conceptions of the economy. These differences may exist to varying degrees but they are rarely entirely absent. This chapter attempts to show that the arguments over tariff reform and empire trade in the late nineteenth and early twentieth century were partly a confrontation between two different conceptions of the economy. My aim in discussing this area of policy making has not been to chart a passage through the 'history of ideas'. Rather it is to show the condition under which the major economic policy planks of nineteenth-century Britain (especially free trade and balanced and small government budgets) come under challenge and that this opened a space for new conceptions of the economy which contradicted, to a degree, those conceptions built up upon the material support of these planks. Looking at this area of policy questions also shows some of the problems with any simple statements about the relation between policy discussions, institutions and 'interests'.

I

In Chapter 2 the interdependence of the gold standard and free trade has been briefly noted. The third element in the 'Holy Trinity' of policy making was the low and balanced state budget. The inter-dependencies of these three elements were specific ones – there is in principle no necessary link between adherence to the gold standard and free trade,[1] and equally no necessary link between free trade and the budget, though of course a regime of free trade always puts constraints on the ways in which government revenue can be raised.

As was stressed in the discussion of the gold standard, a central condition for the standard's working was London's ability to attract short-term funds easily by use of the Bank Rate, and this in turn rested on the City's central role in world money markets. A condition of this role was in turn the position of Britain in world trade and world shipping which was closely linked to the provision of financial services. So by no grand design, but nevertheless crucially, free trade was a central prop to the nineteenth-century gold standard as far as Britain was concerned.

The conditions of Britain's initial adoption of the policy of free trade cannot be discussed in great detail here. It is clear that much of the discussion of this issue does fit into the 'Keynesian dichotomy' of ideas versus vested interests. Thus a perhaps crude but not atypical statement on the highpoint of free trade policy:

> The Repeal of the Corn Laws in 1846, which made England a free trade nation, followed soon after the commercial class gained control of the nation's political power ... the moving factor was the self-interest of those who constituted the commercial class.[2]

Conversely, as Coats points out, 'most textbook writers take it for granted that the Repeal of the Corn Laws in 1846 represented a victory for classical doctrine'.[3]

Against these positions should be stressed the particularity of the conditions under which free trade emerged in Britain. For example the early nineteenth-century movements towards free trade under Huskisson was 'closely related to the problems created by the war',[4] such problems including the adjustment of trade relations following the wartime disruption, and the appearance of fiscal surpluses in the buoyant years of the mid-1820s. It would be difficult to reduce either of these to the representation of 'ideas' or 'interests'.

Equally, whilst the successful agitation of the Anti Corn Law League can be and is readily assimilated to a model of 'representation of the new commercial class', against this can be asserted the 'irreducibility' of the League, its idiosyncratic mode of conduct and forms of organization which had highly specific conditions of existence and effects.[5] More generally, and as with the 1820s, the 1840s provided particular conditions for the success of the League's agitation (especially, of course, harvest failures),[6] and these conditions undermine the facile teleologies of the 'rise of the middle class', etc. which still so often recur in discussions of this period.

One final point on the arguments of this period is the importance in them of the distrust of corrupt governments as an argument for ending the regulation of the movement of commodities. As with support for the gold standard, opposition to trade regulation was a radical course because, before modern socialist discussions of the state, the 'natural' patterns of economic activity appeared the most effective counterweight to oligarchic and aristocratic government.

These questions could of course be discussed in much greater detail than is possible here, but my concern is simply to show that they can be discussed without recourse to the 'Keynesian dichotomy'. The more general point is the implications of free trade for other parts of economic policy. Free trade had from the beginning been linked to the level of public expenditure. A major element in the early nineteenth-century attack on the level of public expenditure was the contention that, without such expenditure, tariffs would be unnecessary.[7] Conversely, once free trade was established it became a major element supporting budgetary stringency along with the desire to reduce the national debt. Analysing the Victorian budgetary tradition, Roseveare argues:

> Hindsight makes this appear to be wholly Gladstonian, but of course it was not. The tradition was shaped by at least two fundamental obsessions of early nineteenth-century England – the elimination or reduction of the National Debt, and the attainment and preservation of free trade. The latter objective required, at its simplest, that public income and expenditure should balance at the lowest possible figure; the former, that there should be, if possible, some balance of income over expenditure. Taken together these requirements hedged budgetary policy into the narrow path of strict public parsimony. Of course other factors played their part ... but the Debt and free trade were the major formative influences.[8]

In addition, the creation of what came to be called Gladstonian orthodoxy in budgetary policy had a clear institutional dimension: a desire to strengthen the Treasury against the Bank of England and ensure that the Chancellor never had to go begging to the Bank. Gladstone, whilst Chancellor, saw himself fighting the 'money power' by a policy of 'self-assertion'. He sought to find ways of making the Chancellor 'independent of the City power when he has occasion for sums in seven figures'. To such an end he created, for example, the Post Office Savings Bank.[9] The Treasury's own central role in economic policy was in turn partly conditioned by the replacement of a tariff for protection by a tariff for revenue which shifted power from the previously central economic institution, the Board of Trade, to the Treasury.[10]

The importance of the National Debt in shaping budgetary orthodoxy was considerable – remembering that debt charges were a third of gross public expenditure in 1816, around a half in the early 1850s but then falling to a quarter by the 1880s.[11] However, the focus here is on the relation between free trade and the budget. Free trade meant that the sources of revenue came to be restricted either to non-protective duties or direct taxes. Non-protective duties meant either duties on goods not produced in Britain or, if they were, then the duty on imports was offset by an excise on the domestically produced commodity. Thus in the period after Huskisson's initial reforms in the 1820s,

> the old system of bearing lightly on an infinite number of points, heavily on none, has been gradually discarded, and for it has been substituted – a policy since carried to extremes – of levying duties on as small a number of articles as possible, and on articles of general consumption only.[12]

On the side of direct taxation, Peel's reforms of the 1840s were accompanied by a 'temporary' revival of the income tax, abolished in 1816. Both these kinds of taxation faced constraints, but these were not significant whilst state expenditure remained low. (We are of course concentrating here on central state expenditure. Local expenditure was growing substantially in the nineteenth century, but was, in the main and unlike today, locally financed so it falls outside the considerations of importance here.)

II

From the 1820s until the 1870s state expenditure in Britain in current money terms remained roughly constant and fell as a proportion of GNP. This reflected the conception that

> the level of government expenditure was to be kept at the minimum consistent with the provision of adequate protection against the Crown's enemies and of the maintenance of law and order; a wide interpretation of the latter included, to the Victorian mind, the relief of certain forms of social distress.[13]

The pattern changed from the 1870s onward. Increased expenditure on both social objectives and military and Imperial expansion (e.g. the purchase of the Suez Canal shares) led to a clear upward shift in total state outlays. Thus, writing in the 1880s, Buxton suggested that 'The most striking and most disheartening feature of the last few years has been the disastrous expansion of the national expenditure'.[14] On the revenue side problems arose from the failure of indirect receipts to rise as expenditure rose. As early as 1869 the Chancellor of the Exchequer had remarked that the revenue 'shows not the slightest symptom of elasticity. Indeed it is much more like the flaxen thread which the spinner draws out, than the band which rushes back to the place from which it has been dragged.' This problem of inelasticity was accentuated by the depressed trade conditions after 1873. In the decade from 1871–2 and 1881–2 indirect taxes fell from 73 to 60 per cent of total tax revenue.[15] Taking 1877 as the crucial year Roseweare argues that that year's budget 'was a turning point in revenue history. Thereafter, social and military expenditure advanced and free trade was placed on the defensive.'[16]

Thus in the same way that the depression of prices from the 1870s opened a space for attacks on the gold standard (see Chapter 2), the trade depression provided openings for attacks on free trade.[17] The attacks were both indirect, i.e. because the absence of tariffs constrained state revenue, and more direct in the sense of being linked to the alleged consequences of free trade for British industries and British agriculture.

At one level attacks on free trade can be seen as the scarcely surprising discontent of those hit by cheap imports. Brown is concerned to show that by the 1890s Tariff Reform pressure was widespread in Britain and this was largely the work of manufacturers who suffered from growing foreign competition, with considerable support from landlords and those agitating for retaliation against foreign bounties (e.g. on sugar). Thus the 'tariff reform movement derived its real strength from the side of industry and it prospered, as a rule, roughly in proportion as industry was depressed.'[18]

Whilst there is no doubt some truth in these contentions as to the social basis of the tariff reform movement, the aspect of more interest here is the space provided by the tariff reform debate for the emergence of conceptions of the economy different from those predominant in the middle part of the century. Free trade rhetoricians like Cobden and Bright have commonly been charged by their opponents with 'cosmopolitanism', a concern with 'not so much the highest development of the nation and the national character, as the greatest possible levelling down of national barriers'.[19] One has to be careful of such characterizations. Cobden and Bright do seem to have had a conception of what was best for the British economy, but this was seen as indissolubly linked to the prosperity of the world economy (as well as world peace). The principle of buying in the cheapest market and selling in the dearest can, if one desires, be seen as an effect of a clear calculation of where the British national interest lay at a particular period. But it did imply a particular conception of Britain's insertion into the world economy, an insertion on the terms of free movement of commodities and capital across national boundaries. This kind of insertion meant that British prosperity would be best guaranteeed by an *absence* of policy at the level of the national economy. This conception was of course fully consonant with free trade and the gold standard. Free trade meant that the national origin of commodities would not be grounds for regulation by the state.[20] The gold standard meant that there would be no domestic monetary policy as such, because domestic monetary conditions would be subordinate to international gold flows.

Opponents of free trade were thus led into constructing a different conception of a national economy in which regulations at the level of national states could be asserted as pertinent.[21] One aspect of this is summed up in the slogan 'Fair Trade' which developed from the argument that as other national states had violated the 'natural' conditions upon which proponents of free trade had based their arguments, Britain should respond in kind. This leads to the assertion of national conditions as relevant only in the negative sense, and evades a direct attack on the tenets of free trade.

A more fundamental attack on free trade started from the proposition that the cheap imports, stressed by Free Traders as the great advantage of their system, had to be assessed against their repercussions on other aspects of the economy. A famous article in the *Quarterly Review*[22] in 1881 attacked the notion of the size of imports as a sign of prosperity and went on to state (p.291) that 'We have about £2000m invested in American and other foreign hands, and with this we are paying for a large part of the difference between our imports and our exports [in addition to exports of gold]'.

Now such a statement was partly predicated on the absence of balance of payments data at this time. Whilst the flow of gold was a concern of public policy, the balance of payments as such was not. As a consequence no one attempted to construct balance of payments figures. Figures were available for visible trade (one might say as an administrative left-over from the days when trade was regulated) but not other items. Arguments like that of the *Quarterly Review* were instrumental in the first elaborate attempts to construct overall balance of payments figures to demonstrate that Britain had a comfortable surplus on trade if invisibles were included. Rather than British capital being run down to pay for imports it was being further accumulated, and equally imports were not being paid for by gold exports.[23] Whilst in one sense one can say that the Fair Traders' argument in relation to the balance of payments was very much based on ignorance, their argument in provoking work like that of Giffen did break up the easy free trade slogan that 'imports are always paid for by exports', and by generating research and data on the balance of payments they did make possible arguments over the effects of changes in different components of the balance of payments. In the same way and at roughly the same time, the commencement of official publication of unemployment figures opened up arguments which, in a sense, could never then be closed.

The two developments are not unrelated. In Chapter 1 it was argued that unemployment before the First World War was seen largely as a 'social' and not an 'economic' problem. Such a characterization, at one level revealing, also raises a number of problems. A pertinent one here is that Fair Traders did attempt to construct unemployment as an 'economic' problem in the sense of a problem related to British trade. A classic case is the minority Report of the Royal Commission on the Depression of Trade and Industry[24] of the 1880s. There it was argued that the great problem of the age was not the scarcity and dearness of commodities, but the 'struggle for an adequate share of that employment which affords to the great bulk of the population their only means of obtaining a title to a sufficiency of those necessaries and conveniences, however plentiful they may be' (para. 57).

The orthodox policy of free trade thus came under attack:

To buy everything in the cheapest market – though not permitted to sell in the dearest – may be the best policy, so long as we can find other full and equally remunerative employment for the home enterprise and industry which we displace in so doing (para. 133).

If this condition is not fulfilled tariffs are necessary.

In similar vein the *Quarterly Review*[25] suggested that the Free Traders said, 'We must, it seems, judge our trade and prosperity solely by a perusal of statistics, and not by a careful study on the condition and necessities of the people' and most important for this 'condition' was the widespread problem of partial and total unemployment.

The significance of this linking of the question of tariffs to unemployment can be viewed in a number of ways. It can be read as an attempt to ally workers with those employers who were in the van of the Fair Trade movement. As such it can be seen as cynical manipulation or, alternatively, as well intentioned philanthropy concerned with the conditions of the poor. Whatever the motives involved, the effects of this linkage are important. By attempting to make the level of employment a measure of economic and particularly trade success, another Pandora's Box was opened independently of whether Fair Traders were 'right' or 'wrong' in their contentions about the relation between trade and employment.

Just as the 1880s saw the first emergence of the 'problem' of unemployment for public policy it was also the decade of the first scare, soon to become perennial, over German trade competition. Much of this scare material was fairly unfocused, with no one reason why German competition was so disadvantageous. But certainly one element was the unemployment allegedly caused by German import penetration. For example in the famous 'Made in Germany' articles E.E. Williams[26] disputed Giffen's contention that a simple displacement of manufacture caused by cheap imports was of no importance, and suggested that for example the movement of steel workers, displaced by such imports, into match making was not likely to be a gain for the community.

Even where there was no link to Fair Trade propaganda the fear of foreign trade competition was widespread in the 1880s. The Association of British Chambers of Commerce, not a protectionist body, was calling at this period for a Ministry of Commerce and protesting against the decline in importance of the Board of Trade, whose President was not a member of the Cabinet.[27] As with unemployment, the focus on trade in the 1880s led to the first elaborated statistics being officially produced – the Board of Trade Journal was begun in 1887. Whilst this did not of course mean that trade was an object of state regulation, it did imply that the details of trade were significant enough to demand official record – and this record then became evidence in future disputes.

Whilst the fair trade agitation of the 1880s and 1890s was totally unsuccessful in its central aims and much less in evidence after the Tories rejected protection after the election defeat of 1892, it was not without consequence. New conceptions of the economy had been put into play during the debates of this period, above all discursive links had been established between trade and employment. These attempted to make problematic both the predominant conceptions of unemployment of the period,[28] and the necessarily favourable effects on employment of unregulated trade. Both these prefigured those in play in the more wide-ranging arguments over tariff reform after the turn of the century.

III

After 1900 the revival of agitation for some kind of protection in Britain was inextricably interlinked with the question of the Empire, with arguments for closer trade links between Britain and the Empire in the form of preferences or an Imperial *Zollverein*. These two questions had been linked in the fair trade agitation of the nineteenth century. Zebel,[29] for example, dates the beginnings of the Fair Trade League from the publication of a book by W.F. Eckroyd in 1870 with the title *Self Help: Suggestions towards the consolidation of Empire and the defence of its industries and commerce*. But the connection became much more important in the agitations after 1900.

Partly this was because of the increase in 'formal' Imperialist practices in Britain: free trade had not, as Cobden had hoped, led to the dismemberment of Empire. Indeed, partly because of the fear of trade competition already discussed, the late nineteenth and early twentieth century saw a rapid expansion of the territory of the 'Empire on which the blood never dried'. Linking imperialism directly to trade protection was in part a matter of precise political calculation – combining the two elements would maximize support. Thus Amery argued that Joseph Chamberlain's main concern was Imperial Preference, but most of his supporters were protectionists or retaliationists.[30] Of course for supporters of one or other part of this combination the other half could be seen as disadvantageous. Hewins, for example, disliked the involvement with the free trade versus protection arguments,[31] whilst protectionists with reason saw Imperial Preference, with its necessary corollary of taxing food, as a political liability.

One tie between Empire and tariff reform was provided by a common foundation in a pessimistic view of Britain's future prosperity. Arguments between Free Traders and their opponents were often arguments over the actual and prospective health of the British economy. A Free Trader like Brassey, in attacking Tariff Reformers' policies, stressed the healthy state of the economy, whereas Chamberlain could allege in a speech in 1904 that 'The effect of Free Trade upon the labourer in this country has been disastrous' and say that this would continue to be so without tariff reform.[32] Equally, pessimism over British prospects was a component of the imperialist creed — for example in J. Seeley's *The Expansion of England*. Germany within this field of argument could play the role of both enemy and model; both reason for pessimism and example of what should be done about it. Thus the popularity of the application of German phrases to proposed English policies — *Zollverein* and the neologism *Kriegsverein*.

Parallel to the efforts of Fair Traders, Tariff Reformers attempted to construct a conception of an economy different to that which was seen as supportive of free trade.[33] (Though here one should be wary of describing the relation between the discursive and non-discursive as cause and effect: each was the partial condition of the other.) Some of the elements in these conceptions were similar to those advanced twenty years earlier. There was the attempt to delineate different economic goals from those allegedly served by free trade. Chamberlain in a speech in 1903 said:

> When I am told that our prosperity is bound up with free imports, I ask, in the first place what is our prosperity? Is it the fact that we are told on the high authority of Sir H. Campbell Bannerman, is it the fact that 12 million of our people, more than a quarter of the whole population, are always on the verge of starvation?

In line with the contemporary linking of poverty to employment, and disparaging the importance of low prices, Chamberlain the following year argued that

> those who try to induce you to believe that everything depends upon the price of corn are deceiving you. What you have to find is employment — plenty of employment and the best wages you can get for that employment.[34]

Symbolic of this insertion of current forms of concern with

unemployment into the Tariff Reform question was the support for Reform by Charles Booth. In the course of an article devoted to supporting that cause he echoed Chamberlain in suggesting that 'The interests of the mass of the people, and of the poorest not the least, are found in regularity of employment more than in cheapness of food'.[35]

In this way the reformers attempted once again to break the interdependence between the prosperity of the world economy and that of Britain upon which Free Traders' arguments depended. This could, as in Balfour's famous pamphlet, include an acceptance that 'speaking broadly, this [free trade] is the best way of securing for the world the longest immediate results for international commerce and industry'. But then he went on, 'It is by no means equally certain that it secures for each separate nation the maximum of well being.'[36]

This critique of free trade and the attempts to set up employment as a measure of well-being led into areas not covered by the earlier fair trade dispute. Firstly it was linked to a much more explicit rejection of the conceptions of the national welfare put forward by Free Traders and 'official' economists like Giffen. In a speech in 1904 Chamberlain conjured up

> a nation – there are several such – where manufacturing and productive industry is at a low ebb, where the people are all either men of leisure, or hawkers, or distributors of goods, or occupying some one or other of the professions which are not productive. You may become a nation of that kind. But in that case how are you going to provide for your ever-increasing population? The amount of money in the banks may increase. The investments abroad are increasing every day. They bring home interest to those people who are fortunate enough to be able to make these investments, but they bring no work for the working man.[37]

Now this kind of critique of the 'cosmopolitanism' of free trade was pregnant with implications different to those of the critiques of the 1880s. Then the popular argument that Britain was paying for its imports by running down its capital holdings abroad implied that foreign investment was something to be maintained.[38] Chamberlain's kind of arguments, and others which attacked the Free Traders' central position on cheap imports, implied opposition to foreign investment as such on the grounds of employment creation. What is of interest is not the correctness or otherwise of such implications from the point of view of an economic theory, but the point that they did *not* lead to any serious proposals to control and limit British foreign investment. Such proposals would in turn have meant criticism of the gold standard, but that bastion of 'cosmopolitanism' was, partly for the reasons outlined in Chapter 2, singularly free from criticism.

Whilst it is necessary to avoid reductionist forms of analysis, it does seem plausible to argue that, in the absence of the social and political conditions for an attack on the gold standard, no 'space' was likely to be opened up for the formulation of conceptions of the economy which would provide an intellectual basis for anti-gold standard positions. Thus the collapse of the gold standard during the First World War and the early 1920s provided one of the conditions for Keynesian conceptions of the economy which contradicted the desirability of the gold standard. By contrast nineteenth-century Tariff Reformers seem to have been singularly reticent about pursuing the relation between free trade, the gold standard and foreign investment beyond rhetorical generalities.[39] They ignored rather than controverted those Free Traders[40] who pointed out that Britain's mode of insertion into the international economy was all of a piece, and that for example free trade was a condition of London's financial pre-eminence. Whilst Tariff Reformers attacked many of the precepts by which the international free flow of capital was defended they made no serious attack on the cosmopolitanism of the City as opposed to the cosmopolitanism of free trade, despite these being deeply implicated with each other.[41]

Another set of problems was raised by the Tariff Reformers' attempt to conceptualize a national economy linked to maximization of employment in 'productive' industry. The conception of a 'nation' thus put into play was seriously ambiguous. Whilst protectionists might seek to construct a notion coterminous with the legal boundaries of the UK, the Imperialists could clearly not be happy with that. Hewins for example defined his 'constructive imperialism' as the adoption of the 'Empire as distinguished from the United Kingdom as the basis of public policy, and, in particular, the substitution in our economic policy of Imperial interests for the interest of the consumer.'[42]

In these kinds of conceptions 'Cosmopolitanism' was to be displaced by a national economy defined not by Board of Trade returns but essentially by race. For the 'Empire' that proponents of an Imperial *Zollverein* and Imperial Preference had in mind was by no means all the areas over which the Union Jack flew but rather the self-governing White Dominions – in modern euphemism the 'Old Commonwealth'.

Thus for Milner, for example, imperialism was not a question of painting more of the map red but 'a question of preserving the unity of a great race'.[43] He could accept that his conception of race might not be ethnologically correct, but suggests that 'common sentiment' will in fact bind those of common (British) racial origin together.

Whilst the period of tariff reform agitation is, after the eighteenth century, the great period of British Imperial expansion, most of the policy debates concerned with the Empire in Britain at this time were not about these newly acquired lands at all. They were about a small proportion (in terms of population) of the Empire, and largely excluded the most populous single country – India.

As many of the Imperialists recognized, India fitted poorly into their schemes for closer economic links within the Empire.[44] Firstly, of course, India was outside the charmed circle of Anglo-Saxon racial sentiment. Politically and economically she was also very different from the self-governing colonies. Constitutionally subject to the Imperial parliament, Indian opinion had been unable to resist the imposition of complete free trade.[45] So, unlike the white colonies, India was not able, even if willing, to offer the remission of existing protective duties as a way of creating preference. Such an exercise would have been pointless in any case as the vast bulk of Indian imports came from Britain. As late as 1913 Britain provided 80.4 per cent of India's imports of manufactured goods.

Conversely, Indian exports went predominantly to non-Empire markets, especially to protected countries like the USA and Germany. Given that the export surpluses so generated were vital for India's payments to London of the Home Charges, British governments were unlikely to attempt to undermine this pattern by trying to force Indian exports into Imperial markets. Equally those concerned with maintaining economic and social stability in India were unenthusiastic about such notions, which were likely to lessen the total volume of Indian trade with disastrous effects on the Indian economy.[46] Given those kinds of problems Chamberlain was perhaps wise in his famous Birmingham Speech of 1903 on Tariff Reform to 'put aside ... those hundreds of millions of our Indian and native fellow subjects for whom we have become responsible' and to 'consider only our relation to our own kinsfolk'.[47]

Unfortunately for such as Chamberlain the 'common sentiment' of the British race did not necessarily coincide with a belief that a racial group defined the national economy which was to be the object of policy. For the self-governing colonies were clearly concerned with an economy defined by their particular political boundaries. Thus the proponents of Imperial *Zollverein*, or Imperial Preference involving the free entry of British goods into Empire markets, could not overcome the desire of those colonies to protect their own domestic manufacturing industries. Their rejection of cosmopolitan assumptions meant a rejection of the conception of a static 'natural' world division of labour in which they would be permanently primary producers. This of course meant the rejection of unrestricted imports from their racial partners in Britain.

The centrality of racial conceptions of the Empire in the debates of this period was linked to the terms in which unemployment was discussed. In the protectionist arguments of the 1900s, as with those in the 1880s, proponents of protection attempted to construct the level of unemployment as a criticism of trade policy.

An addition to these arguments in the 1900s was the eugenic conception which linked the effects of free imports to the arguments surrounding 'National Efficiency'. A classic case in point was Mackinder's work. He argued that the objective of tariff reform was to augment British resources in order to increase the military power of the Empire. This would involve both Colonial Preference for, say, Canadian wheat which would allow an increase in the Canadian population, and this in turn would make possible an increase in Canada's contribution to Empire manpower for military purposes. Equally, protection of the British market was essential to maintain the quality of the British (i.e. UK) population.

> No small number of the unemployed are men for whose skills there is no longer an accessible market. If they emigrate the country loses them. If they stay here their good habits are broken with hope long deferred; they become unemployable, and a burden to the community.[48]

From this kind of argument emerges a clear basis for the well-known attempts to link imperialism and social reform.[49] This does not have to be seen as a conscious political strategy, an attempt to manipulate the working class into support for tariffs and imperialism. Social reform *was* the object of deliberate political calculation of course, but was also notably concentrated on reform of a particular kind, linked to a particular conception of the 'social'.

This conception of the social[50] revolved around post-Darwinian notions of 'population', with the conception (very strong in the Mackinder quotation above) of both a competition between populations of nations and Empires in which the weakest would go to the wall, and the argument that this external struggle would be largely determined by the numbers and fitness of the domestic population. The notion of efficiency then functions to assess and reform the fitness of populations to engage in these struggles.

These conceptions are worth stressing for two reasons. They help make intelligible the particular measures of social reform that are at issue in this period (though they did not determine this), and the way these reforms were argued about. Secondly, they underline the point that the undoubted importance of social reform in the policies of this period cannot be reduced simply to a question of interests being actively represented but was, as always, the point of intersection of a number of heterogeneous elements with no common starting point or origin.

This heterogeneity was also true, as I have tried to show, of tariff reform itself. Whilst the campaign for such reform did tend to gain support from particular social groupings[51] it cannot be reduced to representation of such groups. To stress the heterogeneity of elements which fed into the debate is also to stress its contingent nature; this coming together of elements arose from no overriding purpose or cause; it was not the phenomenon of an essence. The contingent aspect is especially clear with reference to the final major element which both opened up and contributed a constituent central to the debate – state revenue.

From the 1870s government expenditure began to rise inexorably both through social and military spendings. In current prices expenditure rose from £93m in 1870 to £130m in 1890.[52] In the 1890s this upward trend continued irrespective of the political party in government and in 1893–4 Harcourt made a major break with the Gladstonian principle of non-graduated taxation by introducing progression into the death duties. At the turn of the century the Boer War added a further twist to this rise in expenditure and provided the occasion for the proposing of a registration duty on corn and flour, a duty previously abandoned in 1869. Whilst the revenue yield from this tax was not enormous (estimated at £2.65m per annum) it once more put into play arguments about tariffs both as means of preferential treatment of colonial goods and as a source of revenue.

Previously, proponents of colonial preference by Britain had run up against the problem that as Britain had no important duties on produce from the White Dominions (as opposed to, for example, duties on tea and coffee from other parts of the Empire), preference would have to start from the imposition of duties. But the political objections to this were lessened if the duty was introduced for other (revenue) reasons. Heartened by the alleged breach in free trade principles represented by Harcourt's measures, Chamberlain felt able to launch a campaign for Imperial Preference, including in his propaganda a substantial element arguing that such preference was the most desirable way to raise revenue.

For Hicks Beach, Chancellor of the Exchequer, the levels of public expenditure in 1901 fell just short of endangering 'sound finance'. In his budget he called for retrenchment and said that there was no hope of social reform measures like pensions, periodically floated as possible in the late nineteenth century, materializing. Conceptions of the 'limits' to public expenditure are always problematic. In the nineteenth century some attempts were made to measure taxable capacity by measuring National Income and the income of the 'income tax class'. But for the Treasury the main guideline to taxation seems to have been the ratio of direct and indirect taxes, in 1901 'still the only Treasury finger-post to the perplexed paths of incidence'.[53] This conception was based on the assumption that two discrete groups of tax payers existed – those who payed income tax (upper and middle classes) and those who paid indirect taxes (working classes).

The ratio of these two kinds of taxes continued to shift towards direct taxation after the 1880s. Still in the minority as a contributor to revenue in 1891–2 with 44 per cent of the total, this figure rose to 53 per cent by 1901–2 and 57 per cent by 1911–12.[54]

For contemporary politicians the upward trend in expenditure and the rise in the share of direct taxation led to three options. Retrenchment; the introduction of much more progression into direct taxation; or the introduction of new types of indirect taxation. Thus the Imperial Preference advocates could square the circle, proposing expensive schemes of social reform whilst escaping the fiscal constraint by proposing preferential import duties aimed at both stimulating Empire production and increasing the revenue of the Imperial exchequer. From the Tory Imperialist point of view this programme had the additional advantage of reversing the trend towards 'a system of direct taxation which is little more than organised plunder of the wealthier classes'.[55]

In this way Imperial Preference was constructed not only as an alternative to unemployment, Imperial decay and racial degeneration but also to redistributive socialism. By indirect taxes on a wide range of commodities the masses would finance their own social welfare, and in so doing would buy their own immunity from the infection of socialism.

IV

This chapter has not attempted to question the 'rationality' of the Tariff Reformers' programme. Saul has shown[56] that its realization would probably have greatly slowed down the growth of the world economy in the late nineteenth and early twentieth centuries, dependent as that growth was on free entry to the British market and the export of capital from Britain (with a vital role played by India). However, it is far from clear that the growth of the world economy can helpfully be used as a criterion of assessment of such a programme. It is doubtful if any political grouping has ever made such growth its object of calculation, and certainly it did not enter late nineteenth-century debates as such. Also there is always the danger of slipping from using some 'rationality' criterion as an *ex post* assessment of a programme to using it as an explanation for the success or failure of that programme. Yet what seems clear about the two periods of widespread agitation for tariff changes in Britain was that their failure was due neither to their 'irrationality' nor to their location within the kinds of argument I have sketched above. Both campaigns failed largely because of political contingencies. Tariff Reformers captured the Conservative Party but in the 1880s and 1890s the Tories were unable to pursue this issue too vigorously because of their need to maintain an alliance with the Liberal Unionists. Later the Conservatives were defeated in an election at a crucial moment (1906) largely for other reasons – education, 'Chinese Labour', etc.

My objective has not been to explain the failure of the Tariff Reformers but to establish some of the links, some of the lines of intelligibility, within which economic policy was debated in late nineteenth-century Britain. Some of the same ground has been dealt with much more intensively in Semmel's *Imperialism and Social Reform*.[57] My object has not been to criticize his work but to stress certain links which he made relatively little of or which he neglected.

Particularly I have placed more emphasis on the 'economic' elements in the linkage of imperialism to social reform. Firstly, I have stressed the centrality of the problem of state revenue to the regime of free trade, and the way in which the relation between those two elements changed. Secondly, there are the serious but ambiguous attempts to construct a different conception of the national economy. Here perhaps Semmel could be criticized for seeming to push the Smithian dichotomy between 'opulence' and 'defence' too much to the foreground in his analysis[58] and so understating the extent to which Imperialists actually contested the conception of opulence in free-trade thought thereby putting into play different conceptions of the economy as such. By doing so, the protectionists helped create not only new forms of conceptualizing the economy but new kinds of information – on trade, the balance of payments, National Income – which are important for later discussions on economic policy. Thirdly, in both this and the previous chapter I have attempted to put weight on the intertwining of the question of the gold standard and free trade, and therefore the significance of the failure of Tariff Reformers to come to grips with the role of the gold standard, and the institutions that supported it – especially the Bank of England.

— 4 —

Unemployment as an object of policy in the 1920s

I

Following the work of Harris[1] and Stedman Jones[2] we now have a detailed picture of how and in what terms 'unemployment' first became an object of British government policy between the 1880s and the First World War. As noted in Chapter 1 above, three major strands of argument emerge from these two works taken together. Firstly, that the problem of unemployment in this period, so far as public debate and policy was concerned, largely related 'not (to) the miners of the Rhondda or the millhands of Lancashire but the casual labourers of the capital'.[3] Secondly, that 'throughout this period the history of unemployment at all levels – voluntary and statutory, local and central – is therefore primarily concerned with problems of social administration' not economic policy.[4] Thirdly, that the beginnings of widespread enquiry and government action on this question cannot be seen simply as an effect of the creation or expansion of unemployment, but must be seen as the effect of a large number of changes in the economic, ideological, social and political conditions of the period.[5] This last point fits in with a central theme of this book, that the way in which particular questions become objects of government policy is never simple but the effect of a complex range of determinants.

From this starting point I want in this chapter to examine how and why discussion of unemployment in the 1920s became both largely a discussion in the context of *economic* policy and overwhelmingly about the miners of the Rhondda and the millhands of Lancashire, rather than the casual labourer of London or elsewhere.[6] This involves two broad areas of enquiry. Firstly, why did the casual labourer almost disappear as a concern of government policy after the First World War – was this because casual labour had withered to insignificance?

Secondly, how did the unemployment in the staple industries, the 'intractable million', come to dominate policy towards unemployment, and come to be seen as largely an 'economic' problem rather than one of social administration?

II

The contrast between the concern with casual labour before the First World War and the concern with staple industry unemployment[7] in the 1920s may at first suggest that the former had been one of the 'casualties' of the war. But as Milward asks, 'Could the War really have had so dramatic an effect on the labour market as to change radically a pattern of unemployment so long established in Britain?'[8] The answer to this question is no; the implied death of the casual labourer[9] has been much exaggerated. This can be illustrated if we look at that 'classical' home of casual labour, the London docks.

At the beginning of the First World War little had changed in the docks since the days of Booth, as all witnesses testified.[10] Whilst the period just before the war, like the 1880s, had been a period of considerable unrest in the London docks, the labour struggles of both periods had been primarily focused on issues other than casuality. A minimum 4-hour engagement period was won in 1889, but the pioneering attempt by the London and India Dock Company in 1891 to go further along the road to decasualization was largely neutralized by the drift of employment from docking to shipping companies.[11]

A real start to decasualization seemed to come with the war, with the need to list dockers for exemption from military service. The outflow of labour into the forces and the beginnings of registration seemed to offer (at least in retrospect)[12] a golden opportunity seriously to undermine the casual labour system. Registration would only be an effective step toward decasualization if the numbers registered were limited to something approaching the employers' demand for labour. But in the circumstances of 1919–20 with both a trade boom and the return of large numbers of demobilized soldiers it proved impossible to restrict the number entering the register to an effective level. Consequently, the London register in 1920 had 61,000 names, 52,000 in 1925 and then, after revision, 40,000 in 1928 and 36,000 in 1930.[13] This latter figure excludes about 4000 men permanently employed. Beyond these numbers were a few thousand unregistered workers who tried to get jobs in the docks now and again. Compared with these figures the total numbers required by the employers at peak times was around 26,000. Not surprisingly therefore, the pattern of employment of London dockworkers in the 1920s was commonly irregular. From a sample survey[14] it was estimated that 46 per cent of registered dockers were fully employed, 16 per cent upwards of five days per week, 15 per cent four days, 13 per cent three days, 7 per cent two days, 2 per cent one day and under 1 per cent less than one day. These figures can be put alongside insurance figures which show very high levels of unemployment in the docks nationally – an average of 28 per cent of 'Dock, Harbour and Canal Labour' was unemployed 1923–9.[15] These latter figures should be interpreted with some care. The unemployment insurance scheme was designed around the week as the basic employment period. In the case of dockers engagements were generally shorter than this,[16] and the unsuitability of the scheme for such workers was widely accepted.[17] Dockers were able, after 1924, to claim unemployment pay for up to 3 days as long as they worked no more than 3 days in any week. This provided an incentive for the docker to adjust his employment period in order to qualify for unemployment pay, and therefore the unemployment figures may exaggerate to a small degree the shortage of work in the docks relative to other occupations.[18]

Thus the employment position in the London docks by the late 1920s had changed little from that of the pre-war period. The New Survey summarized the position: 'But the system of casualisation has not been torn up by the roots, although commissions, committees and economists have demanded its abolition for a quarter of a century.'[19] This position was reflected in the unemployment figures for London. In November 1929 the average unemployment rate in the County of London was 5.2 per cent, but in the dockland areas of Bermondsey it was 11 per cent and Poplar 9.5 per cent.[20] Whilst again these figures should be interpreted with caution, the position in East London is also shown by the number of claimants of Poor Law relief. In 1927 East London had the highest ratio of unemployed claimants for relief to total population of anywhere in Britain.[21] Taken together these figures clearly undermine the facile comparisons often made between the near full employment of London and the heavy unemployment of the North and West in this period.

In Liverpool a similar sequence occurred. A pioneering attempt at port-wide decasualization from 1912 onwards had been destroyed by the post-war influx of labour, and the scheme survived but to little practical effect through the 1920s.[22]

In sum, the Official Report of 1931 had to note, despite the growth of registration schemes to embrace approximately 90,000 dockers, 'a failure to attain greater positive results' due to 'the general depression in trade which has dogged most of the schemes since their inception'.[23]

Whilst the docks, especially the London docks, have usually been the centrepiece of discussions of casual labour, a much more numerous sector where casualism predominated was building work, which in 1930 employed approximately 178,000 workers in London (1 in 13 of all insured workers). The New Survey estimated that the average building worker lost 10 per cent of possible employment each year through unemployment, excluding the effects of exceptionally bad weather.[24] The average recorded unemployment (1923–9) for building workers for the UK as a whole was 14.7 per cent though, again, the exact significance of these figures is unclear precisely because of the prevalence of casual employment in building.

Beyond the docks and building other areas of considerable casual employment in London included ship workers, though casuality here was in decline; domestic work, where casuality was increasing due to the decline of resident servants; transport work, through since pre-war days casuality on the buses and trams had disappeared; and such diverse areas as catering, piano making and the gas industry.[25] In Liverpool casuality was said to total around 30,000 workers at the end of the 1920s, including, apart from dock workers, fruit porters, warehouse labourers, carters and shore gang workers.[26]

Overall there is little evidence to suggest any major decline in the extent of casual unemployment in the 1920s compared with the pre-war period. Well informed observers were willing to suggest an increase. The Royal Commission on Unemployment Insurance argued that casual labour had not lost any of its pre-war importance. 'On the contrary, the industries in which casual or short term engagements are the usual practice, of which the docks, building and public works contracting are the most important, are still among the most important contributors to unemployment.'[27] R.C. Davison thought the practice of casual labouring was spreading because 'industrial conditions since 1920 have created a large surplus of labour, and, therefore, a large number of men willing to take anything, even casual jobs'.[28]

Precise quantitative statements on this subject are impossible to make, but enough has been said to indicate that the problem of casual employment had far from disappeared, despite its fading from public and legislative attention. Why, therefore, did attention turn elsewhere in the 1920s, abandoning the problem so extensively and earnestly discussed before 1914? Why for example did the Shaw Enquiry of 1920 not lead to any legislative attention to the problems of casualism which were exposed anew – or even, it would seem, any widespread public interest? Considerable public attention seems to have focused on the power of Bevin's advocacy, little on its subject matter.[29]

The answer is helpfully seen in the light of Stedman Jones's remark about the 1890s.[30] 'What changed ... was not so much the situation of the casual labourer but the social prism through which his situation was regarded.' Firstly, much of the concern with casualism before the war was related to its connections with poverty, a subject not previously subject to systematic investigation.[31] Nothing is more dangerous to generalize about than the elastic concept of poverty. Undoubtedly the average living standards of casual workers in absolute terms had, by the end of the 1920s, improved since the 1890s. For example the New Survey suggested that between 1890 and 1930 the real wage of an unskilled building worker rose 28 per cent, and the survey also argued that only a small fraction of dock labourers 'can now be regarded as living under conditions of poverty as understood by Charles Booth'.[32] This did not of course mean that poverty had disappeared in the major areas of casual labour in East London. The continued existence of considerable poverty is shown for example by the information published as a result of the 'Poplar revolt' in the early 1920s.[33] But the previous close equation between casuality and poverty no longer existed. As a keen observer argued in 1922,[34] 'Although unemployment on an unprecedented scale has continued nearly two years, the personal distress arising from it in East London is less than would have been caused before the War by a dock strike or lock out'.

Now it may seem that this considerable decline in (absolute) poverty amongst casual labourers provides much of the explanation for the decline of policy concern with casuality. However such an argument raises a number of problems. Firstly, as a general point, if this were so the implication would be that whether poverty is an object of policy or not depends primarily on the amount of poverty (however measured) that exists. Yet it seems more accurate to say that poverty is a constant of British history, periodically lost sight of and then 'rediscovered' – as happened for example in the 1960s (Townsend, Coates and Silburn, for example). Secondly, such a line of argument would contradict the whole point of Stedman Jones's thesis about the pre-1914 period – that poverty became a concern of policy not because people were 'poor' but because this poverty in the 'ideological' conditions of the time was assumed to have dangerous social and political implications. These implications were above all those of 'demoralization' and 'degeneration', threatening at various times racial decline and military defeat.[35] So whilst the decline in poverty associated with casualism should not be ignored, the importance of this can only be assessed in the context of changes in the general social, political and intellectual climate in the 1920s (which is discussed further below, when the concentration of policy on staple unemployment is considered).

If one looks at the intellectual climate of the 1880s to 1914 discussed by Harris and Stedman Jones and compares it with the 1920s, a striking change is the decline of the demoralization/degeneration ideas that so obsessed the observers and legislators on poverty in the earlier period.[36] The whole intellectual context of what might loosely be called Social Darwinism and eugenics was removed from the discussion of unemployment, as poverty was no longer linked to the deterioration of the race, and no longer therefore had the same significance as a symptom of a general threat to society.

Before the First World War, especially in the 1880s, casual unemployment and poverty had been linked not only with racial deterioration but to fears of an alliance beween the casual poor and the skilled worker aiming at social revolution. Again, this political context of unemployment is best discussed when considering staple unemployment (see below). But a more specific point which is relevant here is the change in London's industrial structure. Part of the reason for the '*grande peur*' of 1886–7 had been because the casual workers were seen to be so numerically significant, making up a major fraction of the total London labour force, London being characterized by a low proportion of its total labour force in factory industry.[37] Whilst factory work is not synonymous with non-casual labour, the two things broadly go together.

Particularly after the First World War, though beginning before, London saw a rapid increase in its factory workforce. Between 1921 and 1929 the fraction of all industrial establishments in Greater London classified as factories (having power-driven equipment) rose from 42 per cent to 54 per cent, only slightly faster than the rest of the country where the proportion rose from 48 to 58 per cent.[38] But this data conceals the growth in employment in factory industry, because the industries growing most rapidly – general engineering, electrical engineering, vehicle manufacturing[39] – were those where employment per establishment tended to be higher than in such traditional London workshop trades as tailoring, dressmaking and millinery.[40]

This change in the industrial structure of London is shown by Smith, whose work is wholly concerned with the new factory industries which had grown in the belt from the Lea Valley in the North to the Thames in the West.[41] The great bulk of the new factory industry in London in the inter-war period was in areas away from the bastions of casual labour in the East End.[42] Most of the labour force for these factories was a net addition to London workers, rather than displaced casual workers.[43]

The implications of this are twofold. On one hand, the spectacular and oft-noted industrial growth of London in the 1920s and 1930s should not blind us to the large amount of casual labour that remained. But, on the other hand, this growth did mean that the relative weight of the casual labourer in the total London working-class population declined, so that the material base for the fears of the casual poor so prevalent periodically before the First World War disappeared.

> The great development in the use of machine tools in the engineering and metal trades had become accompanied in London as elsewhere by the growth of a class of machine operators, intermediate between the skilled craftsman and the unskilled labourer, in status, earnings and specialised ability.[44]

In the long view this change in industrial structure can be seen as one major element in the breakdown of the immensely wide divide between artisan and labourer typical of the nineteenth century, and the growth of a more homogeneous working class.[45] Such homogenization again undercut ideas that the relationship between the artisan and the labourer was central to the political temper of the masses. Conversely, Stedman Jones[46] is surely right to see the growth of factory industry and its social effects as one of the conditions of existence of a mass socialist movement in London, which emerges for the first time only after 1918. In the nineteenth century the diversity of working-class conditions had been one major obstacle to the development of a socialist political movement so that, although they proliferated in London, socialist political groups remained on the whole marginal political forces.[47]

In this section I have argued that the extent of casual labour at most declined only slightly during and after the First World War, and most certainly far from disappeared. Secondly that the whole question of casual labour almost disappeared as an issue for widespread public debate or legislative concern because of a combination of circumstances which devalued the importance of the casual poor, their poverty and the 'threat' they allegedly posed to society. The converse of this process was the rise of a new problem of unemployment – one almost wholly connected with the unemployed not of London, but of the regions of the staple industries – coal, cotton, shipbuilding, iron and steel, woollens – in the North and West of Britain. The way this new question was discussed is analysed in the next section of this chapter.

III

To reiterate a point already made above: if the objects of government policy are seen as 'obvious' and 'natural', then the importance of staple unemployment as an object of policy in the 1920s can easily be explained. Was this not an almost wholly new and widespread problem, and therefore is it not obvious that government would give such a problem high priority? Whilst it can readily be conceded that governments are generally unlikely to be indifferent to the fate of the labour force, this line of argument does not take us very far.

The first problem is that it is clear that governments in the 1920s did not give unemployment top priority in policy making. Whilst it becomes true, as it was not before the war, that economic policies are discussed at least partly in terms of their effect on unemployment, this is far from saying that unemployment dominated policy making. If we take what was probably the most important single economic policy decision of the 1920s, the return to gold at the pre-war parity of $4.86 in 1925, this point can be illustrated.

We may not be surprised that the Cunliffe Committee, which considered the gold standard question in 1918, gave 'only the briefest mention' to 'the possible effects of monetary deflation on levels of employment and incomes'[48] as the post-war employment problem had not yet emerged. However, if we look at the discussion in the period immediately before the decision was made in 1925, the lack of mention of unemployment in relation to the parity decision appears as a striking feature.[49] Sayers has subsequently defended the 1925 decision as 'essentially an employment policy':[50] the argument very briefly is that a major contribution to Britain's depressed export markets was the disorganization of the world's currencies following the war and therefore that the stabilizing exchange rates would encourage world trade and thereby lessen unemployment. The merits or otherwise of this argument are not at issue here, but simply the point that this line of argument is mainly a retrospective gloss put on a decision taken largely for other reasons. Judging from Moggridge, the most systematic and thorough discussion of the period, this line of argument was put by only one person at the time, Sir Otto Niemeyer (Controller of Finance, H.M. Treasury).[51]

One could suggest that such retrospective rationalizations of the 1925 decision as based on concern with unemployment represents a species of the argument that because mass unemployment existed at the time, 'obviously' policy decisions would be dominated by unemployment. To disagree with such a view is not to assert the callousness of policy makers, their unconcern with human suffering and so on, but simply to argue that the existence of high unemployment (or any other 'severe' problem) is not a sufficient condition for that problem to be the major preoccupation of policy makers. For most of the people who mattered in the 1925 decision, the return to gold was seen as above all a monetary, technical decision rather than part of an overall economic policy, which in any case did not exist at the time. This attitude was well summarized by Montagu Norman, the Governor of the Bank, when he commented, 'In connection with a golden 1925, the merchant, manufacturer, workman, etc., should be considered (but not consulted any more than about the design of battleships).'[52]

Whilst unemployment was not of overwhelming importance in the economic policy making of the 1920s, the position had radically changed since before the First World War. Apart from the general point that the problem of unemployment was now that of the workers in the staple industries, not the casual labourer, unemployment was seen as a problem for *economic* policy, rather than just one of social administration. For example, Beveridge's classic book on unemployment in 1909 discusses the issue almost without reference to government policy decisions other than those relating to social administration.[53] Unemployment is seen as mainly the effect of the inefficiency of the labour market mechanism. The only appropriate government policy is the setting up of Labour Exchanges in order to make that mechanism more efficient. The government has little role to play in relation to changing demand or supply of labour. In the 1920s, by contrast, discussions of unemployment are discussions of economics and economic policy. The great debaters on unemployment before the First World War were Beveridge, the Webbs, the Charity Organisation Society and the Poor Law Commission. In the 1920s it is the professional economists, Pigou, Hawtrey, Robertson, Keynes, Clay and others.

Before 1914 economists had no separate theory of employment, but treated it 'chiefly as a concomitant of other problems'.[54] The discussion at great length of unemployment by economists in the 1920s pre-dates the appearance of any new theory of employment determination (the Keynesian revolution). As already argued in Chapter 1, at the theoretical level Beveridge's work was vital in the changing status of unemployment as a problem. By moving the focus from individual character to the mechanisms of the market he made a crucial step in posing unemployment as an *economic* problem. But a large part of the explanation for the change lay not in the field of theory but in broader changes which make unemployment for the first time an object of specifically economic policy. Economists helped shape the way the problem was discussed, but the most important origins of the shift in the terms of the debate lay elsewhere.

A major reason why unemployment became an object of economic policy in the 1920s was the system of unemployment insurance. Begun in 1911 for a minority (about 2.25m) of workers particularly prone to cyclical unemployment, unemployment insurance was extended in 1916 and then again in 1920 to cover the great bulk of manual workers, though excluding many 'low risk' categories, so weakening the financial basis of the scheme.[55] Initially the Exchequer's contribution to the scheme had been the smallest of the threefold sources of income (state/employer/employee). But in the wake of war, faced with the prospect of masses of demobilized soldiers either unqualified for the insurance payments or having exhausted their entitlements, the government first created a system of out-of-work donations, and then 'uncovenanted' benefits (benefits not covered by previous contributions), so that the insurance basis of the scheme was undermined. (The actuarial basis of the 1920 Act was weak anyway, being self-financing only up to unemployment levels of 5.32 per cent as against the 8.5 per cent of the original 1911 scheme.) This movement away from insurance was brought about mainly by the government's belief in the dire political consequences if masses of the unemployed were forced on to the Poor Law. Thus right through the 1920s a political battle ensued over the conditions for granting 'insurance' payments. For example in 1921 claimants for 'uncovenanted' benefit had to show they were 'genuinely seeking work'. By 1924 the Labour government extended this clause to all claimants in an attempt to trade off greater strictness in the administration of benefit for higher rates of benefit and the abolition of the Means Test. However this widening of the scope of the clause generated great opposition, and it was abolished, somewhat unwillingly, by the next Labour government in March 1931.[56] Battles over the conditions of granting benefit did little to slow the expansion of total expenditure, and governments in the 1920s were forced to allow the Insurance Fund to expand its borrowing.

Prior to the war, unemployment relief had largely been a matter of local authority and Poor Law Guardian expenditure; in the 1920s it became part of the national budget, and a large part. By 1928–29 the Treasury was contributing £11.8m to the Fund, but lending £11.4m more. By 1930–31 the former had risen to £14.9m, but the latter to £56.7m. (Total central government tax revenues in those years were £664m and £681m respectively.) Given the contemporary concern with balancing the budget as a symbol of financial probity,[57] it is not surprising that so much of the concern with unemployment was related to concern for the national finances. Unemployment insurance is significant not only as a substitute for action to lessen the level of unemployment,[58] but also as a crucial reason why unemployment became a major object of economic policy at all.

A characteristic Treasury statement was made to the Royal Commission on Unemployment Insurance of 1931.[59] The Treasury argued that the expected expenditure on supporting the Insurance Fund in 1931 'would, taken in conjunction with the other continuing liabilities of the state both for War debt and otherwise, not merely disturb, but entirely upset the equilibrium of the budget on the basis of existing taxation'.

The failure of successive governments in the 1920s to deal with the unemployment problem, followed by the downswing of the trade cycle in the early 1930s, meant that by 1931 the Labour government was vulnerable to attack for its 'lavish' spending on unemployment insurance. The attacks on this spending in 1931 found their material support in the large-scale Treasury payments being made, as mentioned above. One way for governments to pre-empt this might have been to entrust relief of the unemployed to a (reformed) Poor Law. But such a policy would have faced a number of obstacles. Firstly, the opposition of the unemployed themselves. Secondly the fact that any locally elected body was likely to be far easier to 'subvert' into extravagant expenditure than the central government,[60] and at the same time be unlikely to be able to finance itself because high unemployment often went along with low rate receipts – the classic case being, of course, Poplar.[61] Further, the Poor Law lacked the administrative means to test for 'willingness to work'.[62] Thus unemployment relief became organized mainly on the 'insurance' system (based on the belief that such principles developed and encouraged thrift), a system workable only if the conceptions of unemployment adhered to before the First World War had held good,[63] and having wholly unexpected consequences, as argued above, when such principles were carried through into a different era.

Also important in making unemployment a problem of economic policy, was the recognition that British exports were largely generated within the industries that were most depressed. Whilst it would be anachronistic to refer to a 'balance of payments' policy in the inter-war period, statistics of the overall balance of payments not even being collected at this time, the idea of the magnitude of exports as a sign of national economic health was well established. For example, the fear of German competition[64] in the 1890s had led to a widespread debate on foreign trade and possible measures to encourage British exports. Thus in the 1920s economic policy makers could less afford to be indifferent to the kind of unemployment existing in the staples, because of its clear significance for other economic policy objectives unlike the casual labour problem before the war.

Two other broad changes in the context of policy making in the 1920s deserve note. Firstly, as noted above, the belief that the casual labourer posed a political threat was one of the reasons for concern with unemployment in the 1880s. This fear approximately coincided with the emergence of the first significant socialist forces (Fabian, Social Democratic Federation, Independent Labour Party)[65] in Britain. However by the end of the pre-war period it was clear that the casual labourer was strongly divided from the skilled labourer, was largely apolitical, and posed little revolutionary threat; and that

Fabianism offered little threat to anyone, whilst the SDF and ILP remained marginal forces.

The Russian Revolution raised again the spectre of social unrest and revolution in Britain, and governments, especially in the early 1920s, believed themselves constrained by this threat to order. A minute of a Cabinet meeting in October 1921 nicely summarizes this feeling:

> A very large proportion of the unemployed today are not the usual type of unskilled or workshy men, but are very largely people who all their lives have been used to regular work at good wages and many of whom are still making every effort to avoid having to apply to the Poor Law Guardians for relief. A very large percentage of these men fought in the War and they are not prepared to see their families endure misery and want without a serious struggle and even disorder.[66]

Certainly until the defeat of the general strike and the miners lockout in 1926, this fear led governments to tread carefully in relation to the unemployed, though this had most effect on the conditions for acquiring unemployment relief, rather than on any attempts to decrease unemployment.[67] After the mid-1920s the threats to order in Britain are small, and retrospectively one is more surprised by the quiescence of the population than by the revolutionary intents which governments apparently so much feared.

One response outside of government to increased class conflict in the aftermath of the war was the growth of ideologies specifically articulated as above 'class war', above the noisy din of interests, ideologies based on a stress on the virtues of 'rational' and 'scientific' thought. These technocratic arguments are apparent in a number of areas. A classic case is in industrial organization, with repeated calls for 'rationalization'.[68] Also in economic policy making, where a major influence in the setting up of the Economic Advisory Council was the belief in the utility of expert advice.[69]

The importance of this ideology in the context of this chapter is twofold; one specific and one general. Specifically the growth of such views was a significant element in the displacement of Social Darwinism and eugenic views from their position of great importance in policy discussions before the First World War. Such ideologies were also greatly undermined by the virtual disappearance of the unemployed during the First World War, which undercut conceptions of unemployment as either unavoidable or due to genetic and/or moral causes.[70] Eugenics remained popular in academic discourse, but was 'cleansed' of its more overt social and political aspects, and shared in the general pursuit of the demeanour of science. As such, its impact on policy making more or less evaporated.

More generally the rise of technocratic positions fitted in with Keynesian views on the way economic theory was seen as relating to policy making, views which, as argued in the Introduction to this book, have subsequently dominated discussions of policy making. Economic theory was alleged to change policy by converting 'those who mattered' to new theories that the professional economist provided.

This view of the relation between economic theory and policy has several implications, some discussed elsewhere in this book. The pertinent one in this chapter is that such a conception usually leads to stressing the problematic nature of economic theory, but not the problematic nature of the objects of policy. Thus for example the problem of unemployment in the 1920s is commonly treated as given as an object of policy, arising 'naturally' from the fact of its existence, the question being which economic theory will inform policy making. What I have tried to suggest in this chapter is that the question of how and why particular policy objects become such, though sometimes asked about the pre-First World War period, should also be asked about the inter-war years.

Public works, *We Can Conquer Unemployment*, and the Treasury View

The main purpose of this chapter is to re-examine the arguments carried on at the end of the 1920s over the Liberal Party's proposals to counteract unemployment by government financed public works[1] – an argument which involved both the Conservative government in publishing a White Paper[2] specifically as a riposte to the Liberal Party, and Keynes and Henderson publishing a defence of the Liberal position.[3] Normally,[4] this argument is seen as centring on an issue in economic theory – the 'notorious' Treasury View that government expenditure cannot increase the net amount of employment, but only transfer employment from the private to the public sector. By looking in detail at the arguments of the time we can consider how far the issues at stake were ones of economic theory, and also discuss the other general problems of analysing economic policy making that are raised in assessing the debate over the Liberals' proposals.

I

As is often noted, the idea that the state can intervene to affect the level of employment has a very long lineage.[5] However, the ubiquity of the idea probably conceals more than it reveals because 'state intervention' in this area, as in many others, is such an omnibus category that very little is excluded from its all-embracing claims. Therefore it is useful as a starting point to specify the various kinds of state intervention to directly affect the level of employment which pre-dated the 1920s, in order to throw into relief precisely what was being proposed and done in that decade.

Prior to the 1880s and the emergence of the idea of unemployment as a serious social problem,[6] most public attempts at employment creation were by local authorities, and usually involved 'relief' of unemployment by the provision of labour intensive jobs, with wages below the prevailing market level for unskilled labour. From the 1880s such relief works were encouraged by central government, though the initiative still lay mainly with the local authority and the financing of such schemes lay wholly in local hands. Under the 1905 Unemployed Workmens Act[7] local authorities of over 50,000 inhabitants were obliged to set up Distress Committees which had as one of their responsibilities the establishment of relief works. Despite this legislation, initiative still lay largely at the local level and central finance was limited to administration costs, so most of the cost fell on charity and local rates, though there was some limited provision for cross-subsidization between local authorities.

Separate from these relief works were proposals for contra-cyclical public works as proposed in the 1909 Poor Law Commission Minority Report.[8] A.L. Bowley, the proposer of the scheme, differentiated such proposals from those for relief work on several grounds.[9] First they would start *before* unemployment became acute, say at 4 per cent unemployment; they would be undertaken by normal employers and so would not attract the casual unemployed who were considered the bane of relief schemes; and, of most importance in the present context, such schemes would make 'no artificial demand for labour, only the adjustment in the time of ordinary demand'. That is, the schemes were aimed at the rephasing of *existing* demand for labour, with no net increase.

Bowley's proposals were widely discussed in the years just before the First World War. Pigou generally looked favourably upon them, explicitly repudiating the view that government financed employment would be offset by a fall in privately financed employment elsewhere, though he pointed to the question of labour mobility in affecting the success of such schemes.[10] Hawtrey on the other hand attacked the proposals for overlooking the fact that, whether financed by borrowing or taxation, such proposals would only divert funds from private employment creation.[11]

Winch has argued that the Minority Report proposals were embodied in the Development Act and the Road Fund Act of 1909.[12] However this Act was not largely concerned with unemployment at all; in proposing the Bill, Lloyd George 'insisted that its primary purpose was to promote economic development and only incidentally to relieve the unemployed'.[13] To this end the Act proposed the establishment of a Development Board to promote scientific research and education, experimental farming and schools of forestry, co-operating marketing and rural transport, and which would take over existing schemes of government grants for development purposes. Also a Road Board would be set up to control traffic and build roads.

The Act of 1909 is of importance here for two related reasons, despite its major concern being 'national development' rather than employment. Firstly, its tone marks it as a clear forerunner of the proposals of 1929, being concerned with centrally initiated, loan-financed development works, which are seen as *additional* to existing expenditures, and not just a rephasing of a given expenditure. The main differences in the terms of the Act of 1909 and the proposals of 1929 is that the latter were more extensive, and explicitly aimed at directly diminishing unemployment and generally stimulating industry by lowering costs of production.[14]

The 1909 Development Act is also of significance because of the reception it received at the time. Harris points out how little the Act was opposed in its passage through Parliament,[15] and most of the opposition was not on economic grounds, but on the grounds that such a role for state agencies opened the way for corruption. This in itself throws an interesting light on the debates of the 1920s because it suggests that the opposition to government financed works in the 1920s cannot be treated simply as continuation of pre-First World War positions, a kind of historical left-over from Victorian orthodoxy, but must be seen as based on the particular circumstances of the 1920s. (The question of corruption following from state intervention parallels arguments common in the late eighteenth and early nineteenth centuries – see for example Chapter 2 above on monetary policy.)

Before going on to discuss in detail the 1920s, the typology of 'state intervention' should be completed. The provision of work by the Poor Law authorities might be considered a further type of public employment creation, but is arguably rather different from those discussed above because the conditions under which work was provided were subordinate to the deterrent aim of such provision. In any case the outdoor Labour Test as a response to unemployment was widely condemned and was falling into disuse before the First World War.[16]

Finally, for the sake of completeness, the provision of work for those unemployed for wholly exceptional and obviously temporary reasons should be mentioned – the classic case being the provision of employment by public works during the 1860s cotton famine in Lancashire.

The initial government response to the mass unemployment from 1920 onwards was mainly to aid local authorities to 'bring forward' labour intensive projects, and encouraging road building with funds from the Road Board. The stress on the initiative coming from local authorities greatly limited the extent of such programmes, as did the predominance of local finance, especially as such projects were mostly needed where rate receipts were least buoyant.[17]

In seeking to understand the specificity of the arguments of the late 1920s some details of these early post-war relief works are pertinent. Most of these works were set up under the aegis of the Unemployment Grants Committee, set up in December 1920, though this body had little to do with road and housing schemes which came under the Ministry of Transport and Ministry of Housing respectively. When assessing the activities of the UGC the initial protocols of the Committee should be borne in mind – they were explicitly phrased in terms of 'assisting local authorities'.[18] On the other hand the conditions under which such assistance was granted obviously affected the scale of local authority projects. For the period 1920 to 1925 the UGC's activities were continuously extended and expanded on an *ad hoc* basis; as a way of providing relief until the expected upturn in the world economy came about to provide a permanent solution. However by 1925 the belief in this upturn was waning and in December 1925 the conditions of giving grants were greatly toughened, 'from December 1925 to November 1928 the qualifying conditions were made so stringent that few schemes were submitted, and of these the great majority could not be approved'.[19] This change is important not only because it coincided approximately with the end of the belief that unemployment was 'temporary', but also because it ties in with other 'toughening' of attitudes towards unemployment and the unemployed about this time – especially after the defeat of the General Strike in 1926.[20]

So the debates on public works of the late 1920s must be understood in the context of: the defeat of the left in 1926; the failing belief that the export industries would revive; the implication of this second point that mass unemployment was to be a long-term feature of the British economy not just a passing phase. This latter point carried the clear implication that expenditure on propping up the

Unemployment Insurance scheme would have to be maintained for a long period, at a time when the major institutions involved in economic policy making – the Bank of England and the Treasury – were trying to reduce public expenditure. The desire to reduce public expenditure was founded on the Treasury's debtor position, the National Debt having enormously increased since by the war and not subsequently reduced, as in many other countries, by hyperinflation or currency reform. The Bank of England position was founded on the need to finance and convert the National Debt when the authorities accepted that this could only be done by selling debt to private financial institutions, which were thus able to set the terms on which sales could take place.[21]

With this background the Treasury View can be seen as founded upon the relative lack of success of the early 1920s relief works in reducing unemployment (a result predetermined, of course, by the small scale of these works) plus the general opposition to the extension of public expenditure, founded mainly not on any propositions of economic theory but on the financial position of the Treasury.

II

The bulk of the document *We Can Conquer Unemployment* (the Liberal Party manifesto for the 1929 General Election) is taken up with proposals for public works, most to be effective over two years. In looking at this document it should be noted that the proposals are aimed at attacking the problem of the 'intractable million' unemployed of the 1920–9 period, *not* the greatly increased unemployment in the world cyclical downturn from the end of 1929. To reduce the intractable million the programme suggested expenditure on roads, housing, electricity, telephones, drainage and transport of around £250m for the two years, with the effect of creating employment of around 600,000 in each of these years (p.52).

Whilst these general features of the document are well known, other features of the proposals are equally important to understanding the debate which took place. The public works proposals are seen by the Liberals as supplementary to the long-term policies 'calculated to remove our abnormal unemployment in the course of years' (p.7). These policies covered both the international and domestic fronts. Internationally, stress was put on the need for 'international appeasement', 'stability in the world's level of gold prices' and 'ever ncreasing freedom of trade'. Domestically the policies needed were a greater measure of stability in British prices and easier monetary onditions' (consistent with the maintenance of the gold standard), a ising level of efficiency in British industry, and the development of ew industries and the redistribution of workers.

These policies may be seen as just a rather insignificant amalgam of ontemporary Liberal shibboleths and platitudes. But they also ndicate quite clearly that the Liberal proposals did not depend at all n any new theory of employment; in the long run, full employment vould come about without direct manipulation of the demand for abour, by an increasing efficiency of industry. The development works vould serve the functions of both stimulating this industry and ncreasing its efficiency.

The second significant point about these proposals is their relation o the budget. These proposals were to be financed by loans, either hrough the Road Fund or directly by Exchequer borrowing. However he proposers were at great pains to point out that the cost to the Exchequer would be much lessened by increased tax receipts from igher levels of economic activity and reductions in payments of relief f unemployment. That is, the proposers wanted to minimize the effects f the proposals on the budget.

Thirdly, the proposers of the development works were fully aware hat the 'multiplier' effects of government expenditure would mean hat employment would be created beyond those directly employed on he development works or on making materials for use in the works. These effects are not quantified (pp.52-3) as no basis for such alculation existed, but are none the less seen as important. (Public vorks proposals using Kahn's (1931) specification of the multiplier vere not put forward until 1933.)[22]

As is well-known the Liberal proposals were quickly responded to by the Conservative government, in a document notoriously encapsulating the Treasury View.[23] Economists viewing this document have generally concurred with Winch[24] that the 'heart of the White Paper' was the section by the Treasury on the effects of a Development Loan as advocated by the Liberals, with the argument that loans to finance schemes of public works would do little more than divert funds from private investment and at best therefore have little effect on aggregate employment. The view that this argument is the crux of the Government document derives from the characteristically Keynesian notion that the major obstacle to public works expenditure of the type advocated by the Liberals was the erroneous economic theory adhered to by the Treasury, and so the 1929 White Paper can be read as the classic manifestation of this theoretical position.

Winch himself points out that few economists actually agree with the Treasury View – the main exception being Hawtrey.[25] Why did this near unanimity not convince the Treasury? Keynes's answer to this question was to provide one rationale for writing the *General Theory*: that economists who supported public expenditure as a way of increasing employment were not being consistent with their economic theories which assumed full employment, and that therefore the need was for a fundamental theoretical change to back up the economists' policy proposals.[26]

The problem with this kind of answer is that it assumes that economic theory is all-important to the determination of economic policy. If one is unconvinced of this, a different reading of the arguments of 1929 is possible. Forty-two of the fifty-four pages of the White Paper were concerned with objections to the Liberals' proposals put forward by departments other than the Treasury and concerning wholly different matters. I want to argue that even if the twelve pages of the Treasury View did not exist the White Paper could still be said to effectively undermine many of the arguments put forward in *We Can Conquer Unemployment*. And the strength of *these* arguments seems a better index of the reasons why large-scale public works were not in fact pursued than is governmental thickheadedness.

We Can Conquer Unemployment puts forward public works as explicitly a *short-run* policy, mainly limited to two years (p.10). Six areas of public works are concentrated upon: roads and bridges, housing, telephone development, electrical development, land drainage and London passenger transport. By far the most important of these in terms of employment creation is that of roads and bridges, which are seen as providing 350,000 out of the 580,000 jobs to be created in the first year, 375,000 out of 605,000 within the second year (p.52). If these particular proposals are concentrated upon the major weaknesses of the Liberals' proposals emerge, the same weaknesses being reproduced to a greater or lesser degree in the other parts of the proposals.

The Liberals argued that their road programme would simply be the concentration into two years of work that would in any case soon have to be carried out because of the increase in motor traffic (p.27). Yet despite claims that their arguments were not 'hazy generalisations' (p.10) the possibilities of such a concentration in the Britain of 1929 were not explored in detail. The Liberals accepted in a general way that the existing administrative structure was an obstacle to their programme, but by a parallel with Lloyd George's role at the Ministry of Munitions in the First World War (p.6), argued that if the will was there such difficulties could be overcome.

> It was said in the War that we never could produce all the munitions our men begged for; but Mr. Lloyd George produced them. Legislation that would normally have taken months was passed through in days. The present situation must be approached in the same spirit.

In reply, the government White Paper (pp.17-19) contended that even with emergency powers, as advocated by the Liberals, these administrative problems could not be made to disappear. We might go even further and suggest that even with 'dictatorship', which the White Paper alludes to (p.17), such administrative problems would not just be abolished. (Readers of, for example, Speer's memoirs[27] can hardly conceive of dictatorship as simply getting rid of administrative problems by *fiat*.) Administrative problems cannot be solved merely by an act of will.

Such problems in the case of Britain would have included the impossibility of circumventing legal actions to protect the interests of those affected by road building, with the inevitable delays this would involve. Secondly, even if executive power in road building had passed wholly to a central authority and away from local authorities, this would not have obviated the need to negotiate with local authorities over the timing of road building, local town planning, etc. Only if local authorities had lost a vast range of powers in relation to the local physical environment would such negotiations be unnecessary. Thirdly, a shift of power from local to national level would clearly have required the building up of an administrative machine at the centre.

In addition to these questions, which might be called administrative (though having clear political implications), there were also 'technical' problems of a different kind. Independently of the kind of administrative structure, there would be a need for engineering plans and surveys, these being unavoidably time-consuming as well.

These kinds of considerations would be of lesser significance in the context of a long-run programme of road expansion – but it is precisely the Liberals' point, constantly reiterated in *We Can Conquer Unemployment*, that their programme could be implemented quickly. The arguments put forward in the White Paper suggest this reasoning was implausible. Such a rise in employment on roads as rapidly as and on the scale suggested by the Liberals' proposals was just not feasible in Britain in the conditions of 1929. It can readily be seen that many of these problems would arise at least in part in relation to other aspects of the Liberals' public works proposals.

Putting forward as reasonable arguments the positions of the 1929 White Paper may be seen as politically naive, because clearly these positions were part of the Conservative Party's propaganda campaign for the general election of 1929. How seriously therefore should they be taken? Were they not just a rationalization for inactivity? One should immediately point out that the plausibility of the White Paper does not of course depend on their not being part of a political campaign. Contrary to some modern demonology, arguments do not become invalid simply by being stated by politicians.

In any case, the White Paper was not simply party political propaganda. In fact it was largely a precis (with many of the original phrases retained) of a report by the Inter-Departmental Committee on Unemployment.[28] This was a committee of civil servants, not politicians, and reflected their official views. Now clearly civil servants are not political eunuchs. The civil servants who replied to the Liberal proposals were constitutionally unlikely to look with favour on such radical suggestions given their implication of severe short-comings in existing policies administered by the civil servants. Nevertheless the White Paper cannot be treated just as a piece of pre-election Conservative Party propaganda.

Thirdly, and most powerfully, many of the positions argued by the 1929 White Paper are supported by the most authoritative 'independent' assessment of the financial and administrative structure of British government in this period. Thus Hicks writes:

Experience seems definitely to point to the conclusion that the machinery for putting a public works policy into operation is slow and cumbrous.

And further:

even when the works are started there appears to be a technical lag of probably something like two years before expenditure reaches its peak, and hence its maximum effectiveness.[29]

Equally unanswered by the Liberals and their supporters were the White Paper's arguments about the labour market. *We Can Conquer Unemployment*, when discussing the road programme (p.22), stresses that the roads are to be built where needed for transport and not in the regions where unemployment was concentrated. The Liberals believed that of those unemployed miners, shipyard dockers and others attracted from the depressed areas, substantial numbers 'would be absorbed fairly rapidly into the normal industry of the area in which they were working' (p.23). Thus the roads and other public works were seen as having very substantial and immediate effects on the general prosperity of the areas in which they were built.

The White Paper attacked these arguments first by questioning how many of the unemployed would feasibly be employed on public works such as roads. For example it was pointed out that, of the 1.14 million registered unemployed of 22 April 1929, 224,000 were women, 25,000 boys under 18, 158,000 temporarily stopped, 123,000 were over 50 years of age, and therefore any idea of employing the vast majority of these 1.14 million on mainly manual labour on public works was unrealistic. Secondly and more specifically, the White Paper questioned the plausibility of road works in prosperous areas attracting many unemployed shipbuilders or miners. These groups had been shown to be very immobile. Equally, miners and shipyard dockers would be almost wholly unaffected by the secondary effects of such road building programmes, being concerned neither with supplying these projects with materials nor being situated in the local regions within which public works might give a general boost to economic activity. So the idea that public works would have much effect in anything but the long-run on the unemployment in the depressed staple industries is difficult to support. The unemployed in these industries were unlikely to be attracted to such programmes far from their homes, and if attracted were probably unlikely to be absorbed, at the end of the public works, in local industry, given the relatively high rates of unemployment even in the prosperous regions.[30]

As is often noted, British rearmament proved a very effective agency for increasing employment when it came on a large scale at the very end of the 1930s. The stark contrast with the effectiveness of public works is commonly seen as one of political will – rearmament was (eventually) accepted by the great bulk of the political 'establishment' whereas throughout the 1920s and 1930s this establishment opposed large-scale public works. But in addition to this difference, the relatively rapid effectiveness of rearmament in increasing employment was also conditioned by such administrative and 'technical' factors similar to those discussed above. The central locus of power in the hands of national government, the much shorter planning period when, for instance, the complexities of large-scale land sales were unnecessary, and the shorter lag between initial outlay and expenditure on armaments all contributed to the superiority of rearmament over public works in the rapid creation of employment.[31] (This perhaps brings out the particular inappropriateness of roads as an instrument of rapid employment creation.)

One final point on this particular question relates to government policy on the level of employment since the Second World War. Post-war governments have generally attempted to regulate the level of employment and demand not by changing their expenditure but by changing tax levels. This reflects, even with the great centralization of government expenditure since 1939, the 'technical' (and one might add, the political) problems of bringing about *rapid* changes in government expenditure.[32] So even when the political will to do so has undoubtedly existed, it has been found difficult to regulate unemployment by the level of state expenditure.

The arguments above are not intended as a general defence of the policies of the Conservative Government of 1929. The more ludicrous positions they put forward have rightly been exposed by, for example, Hancock.[33] The object, in line with the general concerns of this book, is to suggest that the Keynesian concentration on the theoretical arguments over policy has led to the neglect of other conditions for policies to be pursued. This is true both of Keynes at the time as well as Keynesians writing since. For example in *Can Lloyd George Do It?* Keynes and Henderson argue that the Liberal policy is one of 'plain commonsense' and suggest that Baldwin's objections are based on 'mysterious, unintelligible reasons of high finance and economic theory'.[34] The pertinent question 'How long will it take?' is then answered, somewhat bizarrely, by saying that the government in some of its policies assumes that unemployment will be lower next year, therefore it must be possible for it to be lower next year if the Liberal policies are pursued.[35] This is hardly an adequate reply to the kinds of problem, detailed above, raised by the White Paper.

III

This non-Keynesian way of looking at the debate between the Liberals and the government also makes possible a re-assessment of the famous clash between Keynes and Hopkins over public works before the Macmillan Committee in 1930.[36] Winch expresses surprise that the Chairman of the committee could view this clash as a 'drawn battle'.[37] Winch's view follows from the clear success of Keynes in exposing the vagueness of the Treasury's theoretical arguments as put foward by Hopkins. But if this dispute is read through non-Keynesian eyes a different assessment can be made.

Hopkins argued that the essence of the Liberal scheme was that it should be started 'swiftly and simultaneously'.[38] He went on to point out some of the difficulties of this – the need for land purchases, for co-ordination of different local authorities' efforts, for planning, etc. He stresses that 'the scale of the capital expenditure is therefore not a question of principle but of degree' and that 'it is from a practical aspect that the difficulties of the scheme seem to me to emerge'. It is perhaps because Hopkins stressed so much the 'practical' aspects of the Liberals' proposals rather than questions of economic theory that the Chairman of the Macmillan Committee felt able to characterize the clash between Keynes and Hopkins as a 'drawn battle'.[39] To a degree the two men were not engaged on the same level of argument; Keynes perhaps realized that he was not just dealing with an easily attacked theoretical position when he noted that perhaps 'the Treasury View has been gravely misjudged'.[40]

Also of note in this dispute is Churchill's budget speech of April 1929 coming a short while after the publication of the Liberals' proposals. Churchill's (electioneering) speech included the oft-quoted lines:

> the orthodox Treasury doctrine . . . has steadfastly held that, whatever might be the political or social advantages, very little additional employment and no permanent additional employment can in fact and as a general rule be created by state borrowing and state expenditure.[41]

But this, seen in context, was *not* a dogmatic statement of the doctrinal basis of the government's policy. The passage quoted came at the end of a long passage in which Churchill spelt out the details of the government's expenditure of £300m in the previous four years on development works (separate from the £100m of UGC projects aided by the Treasury). Churchill defended these expenditures but argued that regrettably they had not had much effect on the level of unemployment. He then suggested that this bore out the Treasury View quoted above. His main attack on the Liberal proposals was not on the grounds that they offended Treasury doctrine but because they were precipitate – bunching such developments would cause a boom then a crisis, as with the railway boom of the 1840s. The sensible way was to proceed much more slowly than the Liberals advocated.

The question at issue here is not whether Churchill and the other opponents of the Liberal programme were 'right' or 'wrong' but the grounds on which they opposed such a programme. The opposition was not mainly based on the 'Treasury View' but on the 'practical' problems of implementing such a programme in a short time – particularly the problems discussed by Hopkins (as above). In this particular context (and this one only) the most cogent proposals for a public works policy came not from the Liberals but from Mosley and his supporters.[42] Mosley's proposals have been somewhat ignored,[43] particularly by economists, compared with those of the Liberals, perhaps both because of Mosley's later history but also because he was no economic theorist, and so discussion of his proposals cannot take place on the plane of economic theory. Yet above all Mosley's memorandum attempted to deal with the administrative problems of such a public works policy – the need for centralized co-ordination of unemployment policy, and the need for planning the links between short-term and long-term policy. Mosley's proposals hit as hard at the existing administrative structure of government as they did at the reigning economic policies. Skidelsky[44] may well be right that Mosley did not comprehend the *political* obstacles to such a programme, but then this would apply equally to the Liberals, and in other respects Mosley's memorandum was much more cogent because it came to grips more realistically with *some* of the constraints on policy. However Mosley's memorandum failed to deal at all seriously with that major constraint on policy, adherence to the gold standard.

Finally in this context the nature of the Mosley memorandum should bring out an important point about the politics of this period. Though the Macdonald/Snowden economic orthodoxy dominated the Labour Party in this period, there were dissentient elements, especially within the ILP. Mosley was just one of a group, which included Strachey, Maxton and Bevan, who challenged this Labour Party orthodoxy. In this sense the concentration of the literature on the period on the Liberals' proposals probably reflects Keynes's later fame, as well as his status specifically as a theorist, rather than the especially 'pioneering' nature of these proposals.[45]

The central theme of this chapter so far has been that the importance of the debate in economic theory over the Liberals' proposals has been exaggerated because of a common neglect of the non-economic conditions of existence of such proposals. The precise character of the economic arguments is none the less significant because one can also contend that the Liberals' proposals were much less dependent on heterodox economic theory than is commonly suggested. In considering these arguments some aid is given by the typology of positions on the relation between public expenditure and unemployment in modern macroeconomic arguments.

The first category is the one in which the government engages 'in productive activities which would otherwise be provided by the private sector, so that public spending would simply supplant private investment'.[46] The mechanism of this displacement is not specified and may appear unclear. Such an argument does not appear explicitly in the 1920s disputes, though one might detect its influence in the assumption that public works can never be profitable, or otherwise they would be undertaken by private enterprise.[47]

Much more important here is the second category, which relates to the effect of government bond issues on interest rates, and the effects of these interest rate changes on other investment expenditure. What is of importance in Blinder and Solow's discussion of this issue is their stress on the acceptance by everyone of the existence in principle of such effects counteracting the initial impact of increased government spending, and that the 'contested issues are empirical'.[48] This verdict on modern macroeconomic discussions could equally well be applied to the position in the late 1920s. The effects of government expenditure on interest rates, and therefore on other forms of expenditure is one of the issues at stake, and the issue is essentially an empirical one not a theoretical one.

The Liberal proposals do not go into any great detail as to the source of the funds for government borrowing. They simply assume some diversion from foreign investment (p.57) and also focus on the possibility of using frozen savings, 'that is to say, sums available for investment (which) have to await the arrival of a suitable enterprise to "thaw" them out'. The existence of such funds is demonstrated by the increasing ratio of time deposits to demand deposits with the clearing banks (pp.54-5). So the document accepts the notion of a fixed amount of savings available for investment, but argues that not all the savings may be utilized. Savings put an upper limit on the level of investment, but do not determine that level.

In Keynes's and Henderson's defence of the Liberals' proposals, as well as savings on expenditure on unemployment the possibility of diverting funds from foreign investment is also cited, but the 'frozen savings' argument does not appear in the same form, the argument now being that an increase in credit will stop savings 'running to waste'.

The 'idle balances' argument, though often seen as central to Keynes's position at the time,[49] surfaced in 1929 only to disappear very quickly. By 1931 in the *Treatise*[50] the discussion of the ratio of time to total deposits is wholly in relation to the monetary effects of the ratio, not in relation to financing public works. The increase in time deposits in the 1920s, which was the basis for the Liberals' argument[51] about frozen savings, was shown by Keynes to be merely a return to the levels of 1913, rather than a wholly new phenomenon.[52]

Both sides to the dispute stated their opposition to inflation, and the whole thrust of the government position was that, as both sides rejected inflation, the public works could only be financed out of 'existing capital resources' which were already fully employed. Inflation only recurred as a problem in relation to the foreign balance, in the context of the argument about the possibilities and effects of diverting savings from abroad to use at home.

The general argument put in the White Paper on the question of diversion of funds from abroad was firstly that to bid funds back into Britain would mean higher interest rates, hitting both government borrowing and private industry and trade, and this could only be avoided if 'it is intended to impose a drastic control over the direction of investment' (p.50) which they argue is impracticable.

Secondly, the White Paper argued that even if the government could encourage home employment this would stimulate inflation at home, encourage imports and make exports less competitive. Finally the argument was put forward that there is a close link between the export of capital and the export of goods which Keynes greatly understates (p.52).

Anyone viewing this argument retrospectively must be struck by its imprecision: a list of 'effects' is produced without any detailed arguments or statistical support. This is true also of the proposers of policy. *We Can Conquer Unemployment*, for example, has a great deal of detailed discussion about the cost and employment effects of particular public works schemes, but is content with generalities when discussing the financial and international effects of such schemes. For present purposes, more important than the generality of much of the policy discussion is its failure to expound any new economic theory. The central arguments were empirical ones, and shared a broad consensus on questions of theory which subsequent discussions have tended to obscure.

The purpose of this chapter like the rest of the book has not been to determine rectitude, but to look at the terms of the arguments and to examine the plausibility of the dominant Keynesian account. One may summarize the conclusions as follows. Firstly, the Liberal proposals were in no sense *theoretically* pioneering. Their main support was not a new theory of the determination of employment. The Liberal position was *not* at variance with the assertion of the Government's memoranda that 'the ultimate remedy for unemployment is not to be found in such measures. It must be solved by reducing the costs of production and the cost of living' (p.52). The Liberals accepted this as a statement of the long-run truth, but believed this did not rule out immediate, temporary policies of public works. Secondly and most importantly the Treasury View as a theoretical position has been much exaggerated as the main bone of contention; the tendency of economists to overstate the importance of theoretical questions in policy making has led to understating (in this instance) the much more substantial 'administrative' conditions for such a policy.

— 6 —

The problem of $4.86

This chapter is not concerned with the perennial debate about the correctness or otherwise of the 1925 decision to return sterling to gold at $4.86. Rather the aim is to look at that decision in relation to the problems of conceiving economic policy decisions within the dichotomy of 'ideas' (especially economic theory) versus vested interests. This chapter explores these problems in some detail using the example of the British return to gold in 1925. This example is particularly appropriate because a great deal of the enormous volume of discussion of this episode has employed, implicitly or explicitly, this dichotomy. The discussion here focuses on authors who have emphasized this dichotomy and, in arguing that this approach is severely limited, some positive suggestions as to more fruitful alternatives are made.

I

In the *Economic Consequences of Mr. Churchill* Keynes himself established the terms of this dichotomy when he wrote that, as Chancellor of the Exchequer, Churchill made the decision

> Partly, perhaps, because he had no instinctive judgement to prevent him from making mistakes; partly because, lacking this instinctive judgement, he was deafened by the clamorous voices of conventional finance; and, most of all, because he was gravely misled by his experts.[1]

The experts misled because of the mistaken form of their calculation of purchasing power parity and their underestimation of the problem of reducing prices in the wake of returning to gold. Keynes in this manner constructs an unambiguous agent of decision – Churchill –

and then overwhelmingly stresses the miscalculation of the experts who advised him as determining the 'wrong' decision to return to gold at the old parity.

Against this line of argument the most strongly argued and sustained anti-Keynesian position is constructed by Pollard.[2] Like Keynes he believes the 1925 decision was the wrong one, but he conceives the dispute in an entirely different way. Pollard attempts to establish that the controversy over gold was not mainly an intellectual one, but a clash of interests. The decision makers disagreed with Keynes-style positions on gold

> not only because they failed to follow his truths at an intellectual level; it was because they did not want to follow them, since their interests, their priorities and their aims were totally different from those of Keynes, and, for that matter, from those of the large majority of the British population.[3]

One of the oddities of the way Keynes constructs his argument in the *Economic Consequences* is the stress that it puts on Churchill's role. Whilst this may be justified in a political polemic, the effect is to downgrade the role of other institutions. Whilst Keynes does discuss the policy of the Bank of England in his pamphlet, this policy is treated as a *response* to Churchill's decision. The Bank of England 'becomes interested' when the new parity brings a trade deficit and consequent loss of gold. Norman is pictured hesitating before the consequences of the parity decision 'swimming, with his boat burnt, between the devil and the deep sea'.[4]

This 'ultra-constitutionalist' conception of policy making is not a necessary implication of a Keynesian position. Other Keynesian writers, as shown below, have interpreted the 1925 decision slightly differently. However, by stressing the individual role of Churchill, Keynes makes unnecessary any extended discussion of the major institutions involved in policy making. Institutional calculation is simply seen as a response to decisions made elsewhere, and made for reasons which can best be understood by reference to the kind of advice fed to the decision maker.

Pollard, by contrast, lays great stress on the role of one institution, the Bank of England in the 1925 decision, with Churchill appearing only on the sidelines ineffectively questioning the machinations of the Bank. This approach has the clear advantage over Keynes's of opening up a space for analysis of the Bank of England and its practices. At one level this analysis is forthcoming.

> Here was a relic of bygone centuries, ages away even from th
> Northcote-Trevelyan reforms; a self-appointed corporation
> recruiting its members neither by popular democratic election nor b
> ability and qualification, but by family descent and 'interest'. I
> owed no explanation to the electorate at large; it gave n
> information and refused to provide justification for its doing. I
> enjoyed a monopolistic privilege, confirmed periodically b
> Parliament, without accounting for the errors it committed or th
> damage it did to others.[5]

Whilst these points appear unexceptionable as a description of th
position of the Bank of England they do not by themselves serve t
explain its practices. Pollard attempts such an explanation by mean
of a notion of representation. These practices are seen as representativ
of the interests of a narrow clique of overseas financiers in the City
the Bank of England pursuing policies which favoured such groups
The mechanism of this representation is explained sociologically: th
personnel of the Court of Governors of the Bank of England wer
drawn predominantly from such groups; 'in 1924–25, of the 2€
members of the Court including the Governor, at least fifteen wer
connected with that narrow section of overseas banking and five witł
shipping and insurance; only 2 at most could be described a
industrialists'.[6]

Pollard's position can then be divided into two aspects, eacł
necessary for any serious 'interest-group' analysis of policy making
First the argument that the policies pursued did in fact favour th
group represented – the return to gold at $4.86 did favour the interest
of overseas financiers. Second the specification of a mechanism whicł
guaranteed the effectiveness of this group's representation – in thi
case, as noted, the sociological mechanism of the affiliations o
certain personnel conceived as the decision makers. Both elements o
this argument raise problems.

The first kind of argument raises the problem of whether in fact th
policy pursued did favour the interest group alleged to be behind it
Now this cannot be resolved in principle, it being always possible t
say that if a different policy had been pursued then the interest grour
would have had its interests even better served. For example it coulc
be plausibly argued that, using the term adopted by Pollard, 'overseas
finance' would have fared better with a lower exchange rate. This view

is taken by Moggridge[7] who argues that 'from a longer-term point of view, and even in the short term, a lower parity for sterling would have eased the City's position'. The point at issue is not whether Moggridge is in some sense right or not, but that arguments in terms of interests served can never be terminated, there is always the possibility that more or less plausible arguments will be advanced for a variety of interests having gained from a particular decision.[8]

This kind of problem is usually evaded by saying that discussion of interests should proceed *as if* the group concerned always knows its own best interest. Thus if a particular group articulates a view of what policy is in its interest, and this policy is followed, then its interest is being pursued. While this form of argument may be a useful position to adopt in political discourse (for example, in defending democratic practices against dictatorship and the claims of the dictator to know the peoples' interests better than the people themselves), it sidesteps precisely the problem which is at issue in discussions of policy – what forms of calculation are involved in pursuing a particular economic policy? In Pollard's terms, why did overseas finance see its interests as lying with the pound at $4.86?

This problem leads into the second one which arises from the interest-group style of argument. Pollard's suggestion that the representation of overseas finance can be shown by the predominance of overseas financiers on the Court of the Bank of England necessarily reduces the importance of the Bank's own practices. The Bank of England becomes simply a mouthpiece of a group of individuals – an institutional shell. Now it may be said that this line of argument exaggerates, and that Pollard's position amounts only to saying that such individuals were one factor influencing Bank of England decision making. But if this were so, what does it mean to conceive of the Bank as a representative of interests by virtue of the role of these individuals, unless it can be shown why their (social) position made it impossible for the Bank of England to take up other policy positions? If the Bank of England as an institution was *not* just a mouthpiece of interests, how did these interests maintain within limits the Bank's autonomy and so preserve their own representation? Without the specification of the mechanisms involved, such a line of argument appears incoherent.

Both of these problems which arise from the concept of institutions as representatives of interests can be avoided if we see the general problem in discussing policy making as that of accounting for the forms of calculations and practices employed by the institutions involved, in this case the Bank of England. These calculations can be conceived of as irreducible i.e. not the effect of any representation of interests (or, by the same token, of 'ideas') but as having their own specific conditions of existence in the rules and regulations, customs and practices governing the operations of the institution. The notion that particular institutional practices advance the interests of a particular group does not then have to be abandoned. This is always one possible form of argument, with strengths and weaknesses depending on the particular argument involved. What is avoided is the notion of representation, which if taken seriously as a type of explanation must involve the specification of mechanisms which guarantee this representation – which immediately brings back the problems spelt out above.

II

Following the logic of the arguments in the previous section, this section will look at the practices of the Bank of England 'in their own right', not as representations of something else.

Firstly, what is striking about Pollard's argument in relation to the Bank of England is that this institution is given almost total powers of determination in relation to the 1925 decision. The attribution of this role to the Bank of England is necessary in order to make plausible his kind of analysis; it is much more difficult to spot the overseas financiers in the Treasury of (for example) the Labour Government of 1924 which continued the same policy of moving back towards gold. Against Pollard it should be pointed out that, while the central role of the Bank of England in monetary policy at this period cannot be denied, the role was under challenge. One of the striking points about the Bank was precisely that the movement from the gold standard threatened to undermine this role.

The role of the Bank of England as holder of the gold reserve and controller of the note issue under the pre-1914 gold standard has been described in Chapter 2. The exigencies of war, especially the effective suspension of the gold standard and the issue of Treasury notes, tended to undermine the Bank's position. The Bank's famous struggle over the Canadian gold reserves can be seen as an example of a rather exaggerated response to threats to its predominance.[9] Thus the Bank's practices post-1918 were in part struggles to restore the conditions of its supremacy in monetary policy. The question of the note issue was always a subsidiary one to the restoration of gold but the battle to incorporate the Treasury note issue in the Bank's own was part and parcel of the conception that monetary policy should not be in the hands of the executive. Before the First World War had ended a committee of the Bank had decided emphatically in favour of the absorption of the Treasury issue by the Bank. Such a policy was pursued steadily albeit cautiously for a decade, finally being attained in the wake of the return to gold in 1928.[10]

Whilst such a motive and others could be ascribed to the Bank with reference to the whole policy of gold restoration, the policy is probably best understood in fairly narrow terms. Above all, this policy was 'inspired throughout by the desire to establish and maintain an international monetary system that would facilitate the revival of international trade and international investment'.[11] This fairly narrow conception of the Bank's position is at variance with the argument that the central concern of the Bank was to limit inflation, and the restoration of gold was largely a means to this end.[12] But Sayers's account makes clear that as far as the Bank was concerned it conceived its objectives narrowly, primarily as the restoration of certain international conditions, being sceptical of its ability to make much impact directly on internal economic conditions.

From this concern with the restoration of gold *per se* flowed the concern for the Bank Rate, the central means of controlling gold flows. Because of the enormous issues of Treasury Bills to finance expenditure during the First World War (Bills outstanding were £15.5m in July 1914 and £1098m in January 1919)[13] by the end of the war it was the Treasury Bill rate rather than Bank Rate which effectively controlled London short-term rates. So the Bank, as before 1914, had to struggle to make Bank Rate effective in the market. To reduce the floating debt became a necessary adjunct to the policy of gold restoration, and in pursuit of this goal the Bank agitated for budget surpluses to reduce the total debt, the funding of the debt, and even considered advocating the radical policy of a capital levy.[14] Thus the pursuit by the Bank of 'sound finance' should not be seen simply as reflecting a commitment to a particular economic ideology but as a necessary effect of its attempt to restore gold. Under the institutional conditions of this period the form of financing of the debt had a crucial effect on credit creation and therefore on Britain's ability to restore and then retain the gold standard.

a large floating debt, like a large volume of legal tender money or of bank deposits, represents spending power which can be very little influenced by the normal methods of central bank policy.[15]

As well as struggling to restore the effectiveness of Bank Rate the Bank struggled to restore its autonomy in determining that rate. The former struggle was a continuous one through the inter-war period, though largely successful by the mid-1920s. The latter objective was largely secured by the late 1920s. Obviously this power was more problematic whilst the gold standard was in abeyance, but after 1925 there was little space for challenging the Bank's manipulations of Bank Rate without questioning the continuation of the gold standard as such. The extent of the success in restoring the autonomy of the Bank in its central role is suggested by the Cabinet Minutes of 7 February 1929.[16]

The Chancellor of the Exchequer informed the Cabinet that the Bank of England has decided to increase the Bank Rate by 1% and that the announcement was to be made the same morning. He feared that this would have a chilling effect on trade revival ... Some discussion took place in regard to the position of the government in the matter, and the point was emphasised that HMG had no responsibility for the movement of the Bank Rate and does not control the policy of the Bank of England.

The point of this discussion of the Bank's practices is to stress that they can be fully understood without reference to any 'interest' or 'ideas' external to the institution. Whilst Moggridge is surely right to stress that 'economic analysis as such played a minimal role in the decision [to restore \$4.86]'[17] he nevertheless tends to a Keynesian-style interpretation of events by implying that the key to the decision was ignorance,[18] which can only be taken to mean that had more knowledge and better theory been available the decision would necessarily have been different. Yet does this help to understand the Bank's practices in the 1920s? Moggridge surely gives plenty of good *internal* reasons why the Bank did as it did, and does not need recourse to arguments about 'ignorance' to make the Bank's policies intelligible (see below on the Treasury).

A further reason for stressing the specific character of the Bank's calculations is to bring out what kind of 'problem' the gold standard was. For the Bank, the problem of not being on gold was the threat this posed to Britain's international position. Inflation figured prominently as a cause of Britain's removal from gold. For Keynes the gold standard was a different kind of 'problem'. In his analyses, inflation (or deflation) was the principal problem primarily because of its distributive effects (see his *Tract on Monetary Reform* as well as *The Economic Consequences of Mr. Churchill*) and the question of the gold standard was important because of its effects on the price level.[19] The Bank of England cared little for distributive arguments, so they and Keynes were in many ways not fighting each other but different battles. Their 'problems' were incommensurable.

To argue the specific nature of the Bank's practices is to evade the question of why this 'nature' and not another. Part of the answer has perhaps already been given – to fight for a restoration of gold was to fight for the restoration of the Bank's own pre-eminence, a pre-eminence seen by the Bank as the only sure path to financial stability. But this is only part of the answer. Also important was the Bank's concern with international flows of capital, especially short-term capital. The restoration of the gold standard was not only externally oriented but also focused on one part of international transactions, those on capital account. This means that the Bank never calculated the effects of different exchange rates on international trade.[20] The Bank's calculations were based on the need for *stability* in exchange (crucial for international capital flows) and its only concern with the *level* of exchange (which was probably more important for trade) stemmed from a desire not to undermine the attractiveness of London as a financial centre. Whilst the possibility of 'devaluation', restoration of gold at a lower parity, was raised in the early 1920s both in Britain[21] and at the international monetary conference at Genoa,[22] these discussions did not involve the modern conception of devaluation as a possible means to improve the trade balance. They related to the severely deflationary consequences of attempts to restore the old gold parities. The Genoa resolutions stressed that it was the *stability* of the exchange that mattered, and that this should, if no other means appeared adequate, be secured even at the expense of devaluation.

So, no one in the 1920s discussed the exchange rate in relation to its long-run effects on the balance of payments (balance of payments figures being mostly unconstructed).[23] The Bank of England was largely concerned with capital flows and their effect on gold reserves, with the short-term position predominant. Norman 'did not seem to be concerned with the long-run trend of the balance of payments', and 'fundamentally there was no long-run economic policy apart from maintaining the gold standard'.[24] Keynes opposed the restoration of the old parity largely because of its effects on the internal economy (the uneven distribution of the deflationary consequences). Thus the gold standard debate of the 1920s cannot be assimilated to modern discussions of devaluation, where the calculation of the effects on the trade balance is crucial (as in 1967, for instance). Neither side in the argument over the exchange rate in the 1920s was making such calculations.

A similar point arises in relation to unemployment. *Post hoc*, the gold standard policy can be seen as an unemployment policy.[25] The problem with this line of argument is not so much the problematic effects of the decision on the level of unemployment[26] but the implicit assumption that, because there was a lot of unemployment at this time, any institution involved in economic policy must have conceived unemployment as a central problem. It is precisely this type of assumption that is being argued against in this book. As suggested in Chapter 4, unemployment was a particular kind of problem to particular agencies in the 1920s. On occasion, when really under pressure, before the Macmillan Committee for instance, the Bank would argue that its policies were an aid to employment, though there is little evidence that the problem of unemployment much entered the Bank's calculations. To argue this, to quote Pollard, 'it is not necessary to believe that Montagu Norman or his supporters were "callous" about the plight of industry or the unemployed'.[27] The point is that unemployment fell largely outside the Bank's domain, outside of the calculations of that institution.

The absence of a monetary policy oriented towards unemployment is perfectly explicable in terms of these calculations. One does not need recourse to either 'interests' or 'economic theories' to explain this absence; the calculations of the Bank of England were not the effect of causes external to its operations – these operations and calculations were the conditions of each other, and not reducible to anything 'outside'.

III

A similar line of argument can be pursued in relation to the Treasury. Pollard hardly mentions the Treasury in his discussion of the return to gold. Perhaps this is because, whilst it shared the Bank's enthusiasm for $4.86 it would be difficult to show that the Treasury's sociological composition was similar to that of the Bank. Thus the Bank has to be constructed as the central agency.

For Howson[28] the Treasury is important in the return to gold.[29] But Treasury policy tends to be explained in terms of 'the theoretical views held by Treasury men'.[30] Some of the problems of this kind of analysis in the context of Treasury practices will be suggested as these practices are briefly mapped out.

The central aim of Treasury policy in the 1920s was the reduction and funding of the National Debt, and the linked policy of a balanced or surplus budget. Now, such a policy stance can be ascribed to the theoretical views held by individuals in the Treasury and worrying about the National Debt can be ascribed to a pre-Keynesian irrationality. It is more useful, however, to see the constraint on Treasury practices not just as something existing in the heads of Treasury men, but an actual constraint under the institutional relations of the period. The Treasury treated the National Debt as a problem because it constantly had to be refinanced. Given the conditions of the time, this could only be done by making the debt attractive to private financial institutions – this was the central constraint on Treasury policy. Moggridge argues that

> The shortness of the debt introduced complications into the budgetary process as interest rates fluctuated with monetary policy, and it made Treasury policy particularly dependent on the market, as market expectations of future interest rates affected the success of particular placements. These management problems, particularly the memory of the ever-present threat in 1920 of being unable to meet day-to-day revenue needs at short-term, plus the dictates of classical political economy which emphasised that sound public debt policy required long-term or perpetual issues, provided the impetus towards funding throughout the interwar period.[31]

What is not clear in such an analysis is firstly why classical political economy argued in this way – may it not have been precisely because of the management problems posed by short-term debt? Secondly, would the dictates of that political economy have been obeyed if these management problems had not existed (indeed been greatly magnified) in the 1920s? To put the point rather differently: if in the above quotation the reference to classical political economy were omitted the explanation of Treasury policy would be just as plausible, and the above questions would be unnecessary. Of course it may well be the case that in defending their policies Treasury officials invoked the authority of classical political economy. But such invocation perhaps tends to obscure the mechanisms actually operative in policy decisions.

From this position, the explanation of the absence of a government expenditure policy geared to unemployment can be viewed as explained not by the absence of a 'Keynesian' or any other theory which supports such a policy, but as a result of the unavoidable constraints on the treasury as debtor. Thus Hopkins before the Macmillan Committee: 'But every debtor likes to have his debt funded as soon as he can?' 'I Agree.'[32] It should be stressed that these constraints were not some natural phenomenon, but depended on a particular structure of institutions. For example, they could be avoided if government expenditure were financed by printing money, or by some mechanism which greatly increased the volume of private savings deposited in public institutions thus preventing Treasury dependence on the market. The point being argued is that the constraints exist irrespective of the economic ideology of the Treasury.

Treasury policy was therefore dominated by debt management in the 1920s. Between 1923 and 1929 the Treasury also had a policy on the Bank Rate, and occasionally clashed with the Bank of England over the effects of Bank Rate on employment,[33] but after 1925 these clashes had little impact. Having willed the end, the gold standard, the Treasury had to will the means. The return to gold meant that not only Bank Rate policy but also debt management had to be subordinated to gold standard considerations. That is the Treasury not only had to make its debt attractive to private institutions, but also it had to assess the effects of its management in terms of the monetary consequences, to make sure they entailed no threat to the standard. The policy of funding achieved this by reasserting the authorities' control over credit conditions. The related stress on short-run interest rates was also tied to the gold standard indirectly. Britain's international financial position was essentially tied to borrowing short and lending long.[34] This meant that the short-term rates had to be geared to attracting short-term capital (especially Bill acceptances), and not to debt management.[35] The long-term rate of interest, probably more important for employment, was driven up by funding, but this rate was not an object of policy for the Treasury at this period – it became so only after the leaving of gold in 1931 fundamentally changed the conditions of operation of monetary policy.[36]

The Treasury, partly because of the public expenditure consequences, may have been in some ways more concerned with unemployment than the Bank of England. But such 'concern' operated within the other constraints outlined – the gold standard and funding the debt. The movement of unemployment to centrality in the Treasury's calculations likewise followed the leaving of gold in 1931 – something which happened not because of a desire to make unemployment more important to policy, nor of course because of a change in economic theory, but because of *force majeure*.[37]

IV

This chapter has of course in no way attempted to replace the much more extensive analyses of the 1925 decision available in the standard sources. The object has been simply to raise problems about the way the decision is commonly analysed. An exhaustive account of the decision would have to discuss all the other agencies which played some part in the 'Norman conquest'. It could be argued that this very name exaggerates the role of one particular human subject. Einzig argued in the same vein that

> although officially the decision was in the hands of the Government, in reality the policy followed by statesmen of such different qualities as Mr Lloyd George, Mr Bonar Law, Mr Baldwin, Mr Snowden and Mr Chamberlain, was largely inspired by Mr Montagu Norman.[38]

But there surely are explicitly political reasons also for this unanimity, and these could be explored. For example, a political fear of inflation as a solvent of existing social relations was general. More specifically (and also affecting the Bank of England's calculations) was pressure from the Dominions,[39] who were all committed to gold to a greater or lesser extent. But the crucial point is the avoidance of analyses which reduce policy decisions to the effect of either interest groups of economic theories.

The latter kind of analysis, the 'Keynesian', is looked at again at considerable length in Chapter 8, but it would be useful to conclude here by looking at one further problem of the former kind, the notion of institutions as representative of interest groups. This relates to the Bank of England, a (perhaps the) crucial institution of inter-war economic policy.

In his introduction to the book on the gold standard Pollard refers to Keynes's unsympathetic response to arguments for changing the constitution of the ruling body of the Bank of England.

> All this discussion in regard to alteration of the machinery is, in the actual world in which we are living, very academic. The difficulty was, and is, first of all to decide what is wise, and then, having reached some sort of idea about that, to persuade the people who matter, and whose opinion is worth having, to reach unanimous agreement that that is right.[40]

This is clearly both an extraordinarily Utopian and extraordinarily technocratic conception of policy making.

Yet the arguments against which it is being posed have also severe weaknesses, which are brought out well by the exchanges at the Macmillan Committee.[41] Linked to his stress on sociological characteristics, Pollard stresses the ILP proposals to change the personnel who governed the policy of the Bank of England. Against this, Keynes's position has some weight, for it is not clear that simply substituting (for example) an industrialist for a banker will bring about any changes in the practices of the Bank. Pressed on this point the ILP representative does make a stronger case, one in terms of accountability – the important banking decisions 'should in some way be subject to the effective control and revision and responsibility of the elected Government of the country'.[42] This position at least provides a mechanism whereby different political arguments regarding banking could have some effect, without relying directly on a notion of representation. However what is apparent is that the ILP seems to have no position on what kind of arguments for reforming the Bank's policy should be put forward. Thus the position comes close to an abstract 'democratization' of the Bank of England, with no clear policy implications. It is felt in a rather vague way that by making a space for non-city interests to be heard, this will of itself produce a superior banking policy. In this way the notion of representation could be said to be implicitly reintroduced, for in the absence of explicit policy proposals, only the suffering of interest groups from the existing policy will bring about changes; and these changes, in the absence of anything else, can only be conceived of as representations of these suffering groups.

The general conclusion is that the conception of institutions dominated by the notion of representation undercuts any formulation of effective policy proposals. Reform comes down to either simple changes of personnel, or more accountability, and it is far from clear how either, by themselves, would be likely to bring a change in the forms of calculation and practices of the institution. Changes in personnel and accountability might be desirable in relation to specific policy proposals, as ways of aiding the implementation of such proposals, but precisely the weakness of the ILP was the vagueness of its policies.

In this regard the ILP's position was like that of the British Left in general on monetary institutions – a position dominated by slogans of an 'all purpose' character. Thus as Pollard points out 'nationalization' has been the Left's standard argument in relation to the banks in Britain for many decades, yet the policies this measure is supposed to aid have been vague and contradictory.[43] By contrast, for all his Utopianism as to how policy became implemented, indeed often combined with it,[44] Keynes was always putting forward specific policy proposals which throw into relief the vapid generalities of much of the Left. This weakness cannot be simply reduced to the dominance of the notion of representation of interests in Left political arguments, but it is one of the important constitutive elements.

The Empire and British economic policy after 1914

After the outbreak of the First World War the Empire assumes a much greater significance in the British governments' discussions of economic policy – at least as is indicated by Cabinet records. Before 1914 Cabinets rarely dealt with dominion affairs of any kind; after 1917 the Cabinet spent more time worrying about Imperial economic policy than about any other aspect of economic affairs.[1] This chapter will look at the reasons for this fascination with the Empire.

Keynesian accounts of this period tend to play down the role of the Empire in economic policy disputes of this period – partly, it would seem, because economic theorists had little to say about the Empire,[2] partly because for such accounts the central concern is the origins and progress of Keynesian-style policies into which the Empire does not readily fit. In Winch's *Economics and Policy*,[3] for example, there is barely a mention of the Empire in the discussions of the post-1914 period – the discussion of it before 1914 is considerably greater because at that time economists did have something to say on the matter.

By contrast Drummond[4] has shown how much governments of this period were obsessed by the Empire. For him Empire debates are inserted into the interminable question of the validity of Leninist theories of imperialism. Not only does this distort the status of Lenin's text,[5] but it tends to push policy discussion back on to the unfruitful ground of the play of interests, in order to answer the question of which interest exploited which.

Here we shall attempt to avoid these unnecessary problems by posing the questions, in line with the protocols set out in the Introduction, why was the Empire a 'problem' for economic policy at this time? What forms of calculation were involved in making it such? What were the consequences for other 'problems' of economic policy of this role of the Empire?

In Chapter 3 I argued that the Empire was important for economic policy before 1914 because of its links to the questions of free trade, state revenue and expenditure and employment. Proponents of closer Imperial economic links (mainly in the area of trade) proposed to disrupt the existing economic policy of Britain, and redefine the British economy's relation to the rest of the world. They found space for such proposals because, with the rise of foreign competitors, the gains to Britain of free trade could be argued less forcefully; because free trade put a major constraint on the manner of financing the apparently ineluctably rising state expenditure; and because unemployment was argued to contradict both the Free Traders' stress on low import prices as the prime measure of economic well being, and their belief in an automatic adjustment to loss of employment through foreign competition.

At a general level, the same kinds of problems coalesce to pose the question of Imperial economic relations anew during and after the First World War. The war demonstrated British reliance on actual and potential enemies for crucial imported products, and therefore opened the way for general discussions of the strategic implications of British dependence on imports, and in particular the possibility of supply from within the Empire. Furthermore, the war greatly accelerated the deterioration in the British visible trade position and at the same time undermined some of the means by which the visible deficit had been offset in the past. The War was also very expensive in terms of state expenditure; this rose by leaps and bounds, and though it fell back after the war, pre-war levels were never returned to. A perennial 'crisis' of public expenditure and its financing thereby became central to British economic policy. The reluctant departure from the nineteenth-century verities of low and balanced budgets meant a constant search for new sources of revenue, with trade a clear candidate. Finally, from the 1920s onwards unemployment came into play in policy discussions in an entirely new way (see Chapter 4). The belief that free trade would guarantee full employment became less plausible as unemployment refused to fall below 10 per cent in the 1920s and 1930s.

Initially then, one can argue that the First World War and its aftermath accentuated all those forces which had placed protection and Imperial Preference 'on the agenda' before 1914. But on top of this, adherence to the gold standard became in the post-war years a precarious and eventually unsuccessful policy instead of a seemingly natural phenomenon. This eventually opened the way for a much more radical challenge to conceptions of British relations to the world economy because of the kind of interdependence between free trade and free gold which had grown up in Britain.

I

A clear implication of Britain's free trade policy of the pre-1914 decades was of course a great dependence on imports of both primary products and, increasingly, manufactured items. At one level, British policy recognized this dependence by stressing the need for a navy strong enough to maintain the seaways for British trade. The war, however, brought not only a search for temporary substitutes for those items no longer importable for one reason or another, but also attempts to argue the need for longer-lasting arrangements to guarantee Britain her supplies. This conception is exemplified by the Paris Resolutions of 1916 where the Allies 'agreed to conserve for the Allied countries, before all others, their natural resources during the whole period of commercial, industrial, agricultural and maritime reconstruction'.[6]

Such conceptions of narrowing the sources of supply of British imports need not in principle have had any implications for the Empire. But it did open the way for those who wanted to argue that the only unit which could be guaranteed not to interrupt its supplies to Britain was the Empire. Proponents of this view suggested that even wartime allies such as the USA might not remain friendly forever – and thus commodities such as cotton obtained from America would better be raised in the Empire.[7]

These conceptions became embedded in wartime discussions of post-war policy. The Committee on Commercial and Industrial Policy After the War included in its terms of reference the questions 'To what extent and by what means the resources of the Empire should, and can be developed, and 'To what extent and by what means the sources of supply within the Empire can be prevented from falling under foreign control'.[8] In this way the unavoidable strategic problems posed by war for a free trade country became partly transposed into questions of Empire.

In the pre-war period one of the biggest obstacles in the path of any kind of closer Imperial trade ties (given the implausibility of Empire

Free Trade) was the necessity this implied of creating protection in Britain as a condition for re-routing British trade. Agitation for such protection garnered greater support roughly in inverse proportion to the health of Britain's trade balance. During the First World War British trade suffered a catastrophic decline (see Table 7.1).

Table 7.1 British visible trade, 1911/13 to 1919 (£m).

	1911/13	*1914*	*1915*	*1916*	*1917*	*1918*	*1919*
Imports	731.2	696.6	851.9	948.5	1064.2	1316.2	1626.2
Exports + re-exports	595.9	526.2	483.9	603.9	596.8	532.4	963.4
Adverse balance	134.3	170.4	368.0	344.6	467.4	783.8	662.8

Source: E.V. Morgan, *British Financial Policy 1914-1925*, 1952, p.304.

The overall balance of payments position did not decline as much as these figures suggest because the invisible surplus, for example, increased, mainly through higher shipping earnings. However, figures for the visible balance were both the most accurately known and the most widely discussed in this period, and so the war provided favourable conditions for protective measures. The breach in the free trade edifice came in 1915 with the 'McKenna' duties on a small range of luxury commodities, McKenna stressing that the reason for these duties was mainly the problem of foreign exchange, but also 'So far as the duties do not put an end to importation they may be a source of revenue not to be neglected'.[9] Initially these duties did not involve any Imperial Preference (very few of the goods involved were produced in the Empire) but this was introduced with the more general measures of Imperial Preference in 1919.

In addition to strategic and balance of payments problems opening the way for protective agitation, the question of revenue alluded to by McKenna was also crucial. The war not only revolutionized Britain's external economic position but also the budget. Total government expenditure rose from just under £200m in 1913–14 to almost £2700m in the peak financial year 1917–18 (current prices). From a tiny surplus in 1913–14 the budget balance moved into deficit to the tune of almost £2000m in 1917–18.[10] Whilst this expenditure declined sharply at the end of the war it by no means fell back to pre-war levels. Expenditure in 1924–5, for example, was, in current prices, still four times the 1913–14 level – there was a permanent effect on government expenditure, a 'displacement effect' in Peacock and Wiseman's terminology.[11]

During the war public borrowing to finance this increase in expenditure seems to have caused little opposition, and this added to the constraints of the post-war period by the debt that was accumulated (increasing from £650m in early 1914 to £780m six years later). Thus the 1920s and 1930s in Britain are characterized by a constant search for public expenditure economies, a stress on the balancing of the budget and, consequently, a search for new sources of revenue. Central to this was the Treasury. For them the question of refinancing the National Debt was central to their calculations in relation to government expenditure. They constantly urged economies in expenditure in order to persuade purchasers of the Debt of the continuing soundness of the Government's credit.[12]

This budgetary stringency had important implications. It meant that any scheme to tackle economic problems – for example unemployment – was likely to be the less well-received the more it depended on government expenditure. Thus schemes of public works were always regarded, especially by the Treasury, as dubious measures to be avoided if at all possible. With regard to the Empire, this perhaps provided a more favourable view of Imperial Preference which offered itself as an aid to the unemployment programme but which certainly, as far as first-round effects are concerned, would bring an increase in Exchequer revenue. Thus the financial position of Britain could, especially in Treasury eyes, be seen as more favourable to protection and Imperial Preference than to domestic reflation as a solution to unemployment. Also of some significance was the shift in the sources of taxation. The pre-war tendency towards increased reliance on direct taxation was accentuated by the war. Indirect taxes fell from 42 per cent of total revenue in 1913–14 to 33-37 per cent in the 1920s.[13] This provided an opening for those who wanted to argue that indirect taxation should take a larger share – by tariffs on imports.

Thus strategic, balance of payments and revenue problems combined to provide an opening for opposition to free trade. Whilst of course it would have been perfectly *rational* to be in favour of tariffs for strategic/balance of payments/revenue reasons without being a supporter of closer Empire ties, the question is not one of abstract rationality but of the kind of arguments that were in play and which structured the debates which took place. Within these debates protection was almost invariably intertwined with some kind of Imperial preferential arrangement. Protectionists were drawn into the Imperial Preference versus free trade argument.

Another entirely contingent element in the gains made by protection and Imperial Preference at the end of the First World War was the destruction of the Liberal Party, the historic party of free trade. Whilst Lloyd George could lean with the wind sufficiently to survive for a while as premier after 1918, the election of that year, fought when the chauvinism of war was at its height, brought an effectively Tory controlled House of Commons for the first time since the early 1900s. Whilst protection would prove to be of doubtful electoral advantage to the Conservatives (as was suggested by the election of 1923), other factors generally made them the predominant party in the 1920s and 1930s, and thus made possible some movement away from free trade.

II

In pre-1914 debates over economic policy, protection and the Empire, unemployment had played a part as one reason for doubting the necessarily beneficial effects of free trade. However, as already argued above, the status of unemployment as a problem was largely related to 'social' questions – poverty, the fitness of the race, the need for national efficiency. These terms served to mediate the insertion of unemployment into discussions of economic policy. As argued in Chapter 4 however, the nature of the problem of unemployment changed in the 1920s. Unemployment became an 'economic' problem – a problem related to indicators like prices, world trade, interest rates, etc. This economic problem of unemployment was inserted into debates over Empire economic policy and transformed much of the discussion about that policy.

Central to the case of proponents of closer imperial ties before 1914 was the question of markets. By Imperial Preference the Empire would provide markets for British manufactures, Britain a market for Empire products, and both would gain from the increase in trade. The (social) problem of unemployment would be lessened indirectly by the increased output generated by increased Empire demand. Such conceptions were compatible with the complete absence of regulation of migration in the late nineteenth century. No attempt was made to encourage the unemployed or anyone else to migrate, nor to regulate the destinations of those who did. 'It was a matter of comparative unconcern to the Home government whether he [the migrant] settled elsewhere under the flag or in some foreign country'.[14] (In fact of course, most settled outside the Empire – in the USA.)

This indifference, like so much else, changed with the war. When the Tennyson Committee was considering emigration, the major concern was not unemployment but the need to move 'good quality' people to the Empire. The view on post-war unemployment and therefore migration in general was still equivocal. But this quickly changed. At the end of 1918 British statesmen were still 'suspicious of large emigration policies; by the end of 1919 they were desperately anxious to hurry them on'.[15]

The expectation and then the actuality of mass unemployment, conceived of as an economic problem, helped, at least for official policy, to make a more direct link between migration and unemployment – migration would be the direct movement of the unemployed from Britain to the White Dominions. Again, logically, the migration of the unemployed anywhere could be seen as a relief to Britain. But again also, once state-encouraged migration was on the agenda the way was open for Empire enthusiasts to hegemonize the discussion.

The domination of migration discussions by Empire considerations meant British governments had to tread warily. 'Empire Visionaries' were concerned to stress that the central aim of British emigration policy was developmental. Amery for example argued that the migration policy was designed to 'build up strength and welfare of the Empire as a whole by better distribution of the population' and only 'incidentally and accidentally the actual movement of migration may help to relieve the labour market in times of industrial depression'.[16] Amery could become an enthusiastic supporter of migration as the most politically plausible Imperial scheme. His views were in tune with those of the Dominions, where there was considerable government and popular resistance to the inflow of those on the dole in Britain.[17] The Dominions like Amery saw migration in developmental terms, the terms indeed in which the Imperial Conference of 1917 had supported state-aided migration as arising from the need to encourage the 'development of Imperial resources and especially to make the Empire independent of other countries in respect of food supplies, raw materials and essential industries'.[18]

Nevertheless there seems little doubt that it was the belief that migration could be a direct relief to unemployment that persuaded the government to put money into aiding migration from 1922.[19] Whilst the results of the Empire Settlement Act of that year were disappointing to its supporters the principle of state-aided emigration was established, (partly because of dominion pressure) and despite Treasury objections.[20] In this, as in other areas, governments had recognized an economic problem called unemployment, and had attempted to diminish it – before any revolution in what economic theorists were saying about unemployment.

In addition to migration another new area of state regulation in favour of the Empire was overseas investment. Before 1914 capital, like migrants, had been allowed with few exceptions to flow where it would. In the case of investment, as with trade, the initial impetus to control came not at all from Imperial designs but from a perceived need for regulation *per se*, which regulation was then modified in favour of the Empire. Regulation was introduced for two reasons – to aid the exchange rate of the pound in order to protect the Bank of England's gold reserve, and to aid the Government's loan operations – in modern terms to prevent the government being 'crowded out' by foreign issues.[21] The Treasury consented to the relaxation of controls in favour of the Empire, mainly, it would seem, because they felt Empire countries were more likely to spend the receipts from British loans on British exports. But here, as with the case of migration, the Treasury put other priorities before the Empire. In 1925 the policy of returning to gold led to pressure to embargo loans even to the Colonies and Dominions and, despite Amery's objections, this was done albeit briefly.[22]

The general argument so far is that the importance of the Empire in economic policy discussions in the war and early post-war period was the effect of a range of heterogeneous elements which opened the way for regulation of the economy in a variety of ways. The general domination of 'regulatory' discussions by Empire concerns, and the particular fact of the strength of Empire Visionaries in a revived Tory party meant that the pressures for regulation were channelled into giving preference – in trade, migration and investment – to the Empire.

To stress the revival of Empire 'sentiment' may therefore be at one level misleading. The war had, in a range of ways, undermined the conditions of existence of the pre-war structure of economic policy. The Empire was then spatchcocked onto the regulatory pattern which grew up in an *ad hoc* way in the wake of this undermining. But, as already suggested, this can be explained by the fact that the only pro-regulatory discourse on economic policy in existence was that which was pro-Imperial. Willy nilly those who wanted to regulate were forced into the arms of imperialists such as Amery and Hewins.

Perhaps the Imperialists implicitly recognized the contingent nature of their successes by the way they stressed that element of the Imperial design which fitted current concerns. In the pre-war arguments they had stressed the role of trade, of Imperial Preference, at a time when British trade was becoming an object of concern in the face of increased competition. After 1914 the general change in the significance of unemployment problem meant that Empire migration and its direct or, more usually, indirect effects on unemployment were pushed to the fore. Investment in the Empire was also proposed as a relief to unemployment in Britain. Neither of these things had been of any significance in the earlier Imperial argument.

Finally on this point a clear similarity between the pre- and post-war discussions of Empire economic policy should be noted. This is that the 'Empire' under discussion was overwhelmingly the White Dominions. A few loans might be made for the development of the Colonies on the grounds of Imperial self-sufficiency and/or its effects on employment, but the sums involved were usually trivial – and these loans were not entirely immune from the periodic attempts to prune expenditure. Above all, India was largely excluded from these discussions. Imperial trade preference never made much sense for India, and in any case she was granted tariff autonomy effectively in 1919, and this led to protection of 'infant' industries precisely in those areas where Britain exported most to India – cottons and iron and steel. India also had no interest in the newly important Empire question – migration. This was quite explicitly concerned with *white* people: 'The object of Empire settlement is to distribute the white population of the British commonwealth in the most efficient manner as between all its parts.'[23] Indeed, in her relations with the Empire at this time India was concerned mostly with the racist practices of the White Dominions in general and South Africa in particular. It was not only for Beaverbrook that the Empire of this period 'was an association of free British communities rather than the Indian and colonial Empire of exploitation.'[24]

III

We have stressed the contingent nature of the revival of Imperial sentiment in the war and post-war years. Empire enthusiasts like Hewins who felt initially that the struggle had been won, soon felt that somehow the situation was drifting away from them. By 1922, he recorded,[25] Bonar Law, the Premier, was arguing that no further change in the fiscal system was possible because this would undermine confidence, a confidence already hit by the fluctuations of sterling. The *Round Table*[26] might still believe that the imperialists' seventh heaven of Empire free trade was practicable, but generally by 1923, and especially after the election of that year, the Empire enthusiasts were on the defensive. Amery[27] argues that, after the election, Baldwin's 'overriding preoccupation was to hold his party together. As a result his approach to the fiscal question became increasingly Balfourian. In principle he was a tariff reformer; in practice he acted as a brake on the policy.' The Labour government's repeal of some preferential duties, the failure of imperial migration to match up to expectations, and the continuing lack of enthusiasm of the Treasury for imperial expenditure adds weight to the argument that by the mid-1920s the factors which had brought Empire questions to the fore were lessening their force. The budget was in surplus, the balance of payments relatively healthy (even if at the cost of deflation) and strategic arguments no longer appeared pressing.[28]

By the late 1920s in Britain it could be said that whilst a number of Imperial concerns had been taken on board in policy making, they were far from central. Even at the Imperial Conferences, like that of 1926, constitutional issues took precedence, with economic questions discussed in fairly ritual fashion. Thus the revolution in fiscal policy which occurred in 1931 is best seen as not in any sense a culmination of previous pressures for protection and imperial preference. As with the First World War, the events of the early 1930s generated a complexity of circumstances which provided the Imperial Visionaries and their allies with an opportunity once again to mould events to their liking.

By 1931 both the balance of trade and the budget were once again deteriorating in the face of world depression. Keynes and his allies on the Macmillan Committee[29] proposed to attack both of these problems, as well as that of business confidence, by a 10 per cent 'revenue' tariff. Such proposals would possibly have remained a dead letter without the political events of the late summer and autumn of 1931 which brought a National (i.e. Conservative) government to power. Following from the election pledges made in 1931 Neville Chamberlain, the Chancellor of the Exchequer, introduced a measure of general protection in the beginning of 1932.

In his speech Chamberlain put forward seven reasons for introducing protection.[30] Working with implied order of priority he gave these as the balance of trade, revenue, the prevention of a rise in the cost of living following depreciation, increased employment, the encouragement of industrial efficiency, bargaining with foreign countries, and finally its use as a measure of Imperial Preference. This list was clearly a catch all, aimed at securing the maximum of support for his proposals. But it is clear, both from this list and at other points in his speech, that the central reasons for introducing protection were revenue and the balance of payments. (Though of course there was a trade-off between these objectives which Chamberlain did not make clear – the more the tariff restricted imports the less the revenue, and vice versa.)

Two points about this protective policy appear important. First the break with the past was inconceivable without first 'going off Gold'. The whole strategy of the Bank of England and the Treasury in the 1920s was based on the assumption that adherence to gold was central to the recovery and growth of world and therefore British trade. Once this policy proved impossible, the influence of those institutions was to a degree undermined. More specifically the constraint imposed by the need to maintain the parity of the pound also disappeared; not only was internal policy no longer so constrained, but also within the external accounts attention now focused directly on the trade and capital accounts and not on the gold flows. The former allowed the pursuit of a cheap money policy; the latter created a balance of payments problem in something like the modern sense. Thus the (forced) departure from gold effected a fundamental severance in economic policy. Domestic policies could be pursued, the economy could be 'managed' in the sense of using monetary or other policy relatively free from the constraint of international flows of gold. Internationally also a whole new area of policy was opened up – the level of the exchange rate, for example, becoming in itself an object of policy rather than simply something to be defended.

Secondly, the protection of Britain opened the way for 'managing' the economy in another sense. This was not the Keynesian sense of attempting to regulate the level of aggregate demand, but attempting to create a market via protection in which 'rationalized' industry could find an outlet for its product. Thus Amery spoke of the necessity of Imperial Preference 'because the development of modern science and machinery necessitates larger economic units. Rationalization, to use the popular catchword, is the need of the day, in every aspect of life.'[31] This led to the use of tariffs to bargain within Britain, with industries which would be offered increased tariffs in return for reorganization of their structure and internal organization. These bargains may not have been successful, but it is surely only in Keynesian retrospect that one can assert, as do Howson and Winch, 'Nor can the steps taken in these industries be regarded as innovations in economic management'.[32] For, in relation to the problems as they were posed at the time, such policies are just as significant as those which can be constructed as precursors of Keynesian-style economic management.

Chamberlain in his speech introducing the tariffs described his proposals as the 'direct and legitimate descendant' of those of his father, Joseph Chamberlain. But it is clear that the conditions of existence of the protective policy were wholly contingent i.e. were not produced by enthusiasm for Empire. The forced departure from gold, the search for revenue and relief of balance of payments problems, like the First World War, created a space for Imperial Preference to be 'tacked on' to protective measures.

In this light, the Ottawa negotiations and agreements of 1931 can best be understood.

> The British leaders had not come to the conference table as missionaries of Empire. They had been driven to it by an unprecedented economic and financial crisis which had shattered Britain's established fiscal system and created nearly 3m unemployed.[33]

The great stumbling block on the British side to a policy of Imperial Preference had of course always been the objection to taxing foods. The depression of the early 1930s lessened this objection by bringing to the fore the question of domestic agriculture. Traditionally, imperial enthusiasts had argued the need to expand British agriculture from its uniquely small part in the economy.[34] But after 1929 the question rapidly became the shrinking of agriculture in the face of the collapse of international prices. The problem for the Dominions then became not inducing Britain to protect, but how far that protection would be against Dominion as well as foreign producers. Under Australasian pressure the Dominions were successful in putting the main burden of the tariffs on non-Empire producers.[35]

The Ottawa conference was not, then, a sign of the recrudescence of imperial sentiment so much as a further confirmation that the arguments about 'Empire' could be linked to the central concerns of British external economic policy. These concerns were above all dominated by the search for markets. Men and money were displaced in imperial concerns by markets, but as part and parcel of a general concern with finding outlets for British products. After Ottawa the Empire became just another part of the general bi-lateral trade bargaining system.[36] In a sense this was just pursuing the logic of the breakdown of the free trade system. A strongly anti-Empire writer like Fay[37] followed this logic in arguing that if Britain was going to have tariffs then one might as well have Ottawa-style arrangements; in the absence of free trade it makes sense to bargain with your suppliers.

IV

Discussions of Empire economic policy were important because of the way they hegemonized discussion of policy. This may tend to disguise the fact that what was often at stake in such discussions was not so much British economic relations with the Empire, but Britain's relation to the world economy as a whole and the implications of that for domestic economic policy. Those heterogeneous conditions which allowed for discussion of questions of Empire were at the same time opening a space for discussions of management and regulation of the economy, the two things were inextricable. The Empire was posed as the solution to the economic problems which British governments concerned themselves with after 1914 – problems which either had not existed for the authorities, or existed in an entirely different form, in the unregulated economy before 1914. Empire enthusiasts produced a conception of national economy within which these problems could be located, and proposed that only the Empire could solve these national problems. Thus Amery in 1924[38] argued that 'Empire development is thus the true key to the solution of our economic problems, both of those arising from the impoverishment and confusion of Europe and of those arising from our Debt to America'.

The contingent nature of the obsession with Empire in Britain in this period has been and should be stressed. The effects of this in helping to open up the question of the regulation and management of the economy must likewise be emphasized. This emphasis does not fit into the teleologies of the 'rise of Keynesianism' which often dominate discussion of this period, and we are therefore better equipped to understand the full complexities involved in the creation of 'problems' for economic policy.

British economic policy 1931–45:
a Keynesian revolution?

In a famous article R.C.O. Matthews asked why it was that between 1945 and the late 1960s Britain had full employment.[1] He suggested that if asked this question

> most people would tend to reply, without thinking very much, that it is because we have had a full-employment policy – we have had the Keynesian revolution. Now supposing this were the right answer, it would be a remarkable thing. It would mean that the most important single feature of the post-war British economy has been due to an advance in economic theory. It would be a most striking vindication of Keynes' celebrated dictum about the ultimate primacy of abstract thought in the world of affairs.

Matthews then goes on to argue that in any simple sense full employment in Britain after the Second World War has not been the result of Keynesian policies, but above all of the higher level of investment. Fiscal policy has been a matter of varying the size of the current account *surplus* (this only changed in the calendar year 1975, when for the first time a deficit was recorded)[2] and has therefore been deflationary. The argument presented by Matthews is a radical challenge to much discussion of British economic policy since 1945. In this final chapter I want to extend this challenge to the way in which British economic policy from 1931 to 1945 is commonly conceived, a conception which is equally Keynesian in the sense of the Matthews quotation above and in many ways equally problematic.

Whilst budgetary policy for most of the period after 1945 may have been deflationary, nevertheless by the late 1940s there had clearly been a radical change of some sort in such policy compared with the beginning of the 1930s. Budgetary policy was used to try and affect the level of employment in a way unheard of a decade and a half earlier. On this point one has to be careful: it would be mistaken to argue that budgetary policy was unconditionally subordinated to the level of employment. By this is meant not only the obvious point that as full employment was approached the deterioration in the balance of payments led to policies which had the effect of decreasing employment, but also that the use of the budget to regulate employment was conditional on a generally high level of employment caused by high investment and buoyant world trade. If these factors had been absent, as they were in the mid-1970s, any attempt to bring employment up to anything approaching 'full' would have required massive budget deficits. It is very doubtful if such deficits would ever be forthcoming as, in British institutional conditions, they always have to be financed by private institutions and therefore have to be sold on terms which those institutions deem to be acceptable. The City has the ability, which flows from this, to constrain a government's deficit. In 1976 for instance, the scale of government borrowing was held to threaten financial stability, and this led to a 'gilt strike' in the summer of that year.

If budget deficits are so constrained, it follows that the pursuit of a Keynesian full employment policy is only possible at relatively low levels of unemployment as determined by world trade conditions and private investment. An example might be economic policy up to the late 1960s when at worst only a small budget deficit was required to promote full employment. So, when looking at policy changes in Britain 1931–45 one has to make clear in advance what is to be explained. The problem is not how policy changed so radically that on its own it made possible the achievement of full employment when applied in the post-war period, but how it changed to make possible the use of budget deficits to regulate employment *within fairly narrow parameters*.

Many authors have attempted to explain these changes. The predominant explanation has been extremely Keynesian. A typical example is Michael Stewart:

> Despite dire predictions in 1945, Britain has now enjoyed full employment for a quarter of a century. Such a tremendous transformation might be expected to have many causes. But in this case one can point to one cause above all others: the publication in 1936 of a book called the *General Theory* by John Maynard Keynes.[3]

A similar argument for America is made by Lekachman, who appropriately heads his chapter on the adoption of Keynesian policies in the USA 'The Triumph of an Idea'.[4] These authors were writing before recent attacks on Keynesianism gained strength, and so may be thought to be rather dead dogs. However a feature of these attacks has been in many cases, a simple reversal of terms. Keynes's theory is changed from the root of all good to the root of most evil. Thus for the 'New Right', Keynes is credited with having destroyed the constraints on unbalanced budgets and thus opened the way to all the horrors of the modern world.[5]

Historians of economic policy have pursued a broadly similar line of stress on the role of Keynes's theory in changing economic policy. Winch, for example, argues that 'the third phase opened with the Second World War and has continued roughly to the present day. It was during this period that the Keynesian revolution in thought was carried into the realm of policy.'[6] Howson and Winch pursue a similar line of thought.[7] The rationale of their book is that the reports of the Economic Advisory Council had effects 'by no means negligible' on policy makers in the Treasury, and therefore acted as a kind of conduit for the flow of Keynesian thought into the centres of policy decision. Thus, for example, by 1940 Hopkins of the Treasury had been converted to Keynesianism and this was significant for wartime changes in economic policy.[8] Finally, Howson is concerned with 'the consequences of the theoretical views held by the Treasury men'[9] and this concern derives its pertinence from the belief that the changes in the views of the Treasury men were important in moving towards economic management on Keynesian principles.[10]

Against these positions, the argument of this Chapter is that the pursuit of a Keynesian policy (in the narrow sense defined above) was premised on a range of specific factors without which such a policy change would have been inconceivable.[11] The factors which will be concentrated on here are the departure from the gold standard, the growth of government expenditure, the development of national income accounting, and the political circumstances of the Second World War.

I

In principle, adherence to a gold standard means that a nationally oriented monetary policy is impossible, because such a policy must always be subordinated to the international flow of gold. Inflows and outflows of gold determine the money supply or, more relevantly in the case of pre-1914 Britain, lead directly to interest rate changes with the money supply controlled to make those rate changes effective. If gold does not form the sole medium of internal circulation the linkage between the international flow of gold and the internal circulation is necessarily mediated by, for example, the reserve requirements for the issue of non-gold money. Given this condition a country can be on the gold standard but still have room for manoeuvre. The amount of such room obviously varies.

In the USA in the 1920s there was considerable room because the country ran a constant payments surplus and so accumulated gold. This gold was mostly 'sterilized', i.e. not allowed to form the basis for an extension of the US domestic money supply. This was a perfectly plausible (if perhaps in the long run, self-defeating) policy to pursue, insulating the domestic economy from international pressure. The UK case was clearly different. With small reserves and a constant tendency to lose gold[12] the authorities were very much constrained by the adherence to gold. This constraint was not absolute: the Bank of England, like the Federal Reserve in the USA, did cushion the effects of gold flows in the 1920s. As Keynes recognized early in the 1920s, though committed to gold the Bank was not simply a passive reactor to gold flow.

> If we restore the gold standard ... are we to continue and develop the experimental innovations of our present policy, ignoring the 'bank rate' and, if necessary, allow unmoved a piling up of gold reserves for beyond our requirements or their depletion for below them?[13] The answer to this question was 'yes', as the Macmillan Report recognized.[14]

However, the limits of manoeuvre were narrow and retention of gold meant, in particular, relatively high interest rates in the late 1920s.[15] For Britain, therefore, going off gold removed a significant constraint on monetary policy. This was not a move from total constraint to total freedom, but it was none the less important. After September 1931, as Nevin remarks, the 'authorities were in fact facing for the first time the problem of a conscious and active monetary policy'.[16] Previously the question had been 'how far, for given special reasons, should policy diverge from the clearly indicated gold-standard path?' After that date the question concerned what policy was to be – especially because the external position was, like that of the USA in the 1920s, showing a constant tendency to surplus and the accumulation of gold. So far, the departure from gold has been stressed as making space for a new kind of *monetary* policy. But more generally, departure from gold in the British conditions of the 1930s gave space for a number of conceptions of a *national* economy to grow up, because, with the insulation from the world economy, manipulation of an economy at the level of the nation state became much more plausible. Thus in the 1930s there were a large number of commentators who tried to outline how the British economy could be improved in a variety of directions. Not all of these were new but what was innovative was the focus on internal conditions, and the decline in interest in external.[17] (Though for Imperialists 'internal' would include the White Empire – see Chapter 7.) Articulated with these arguments are the beginnings of 'management' of the economy in the modern sense – specifically the cheap money policy.[18]

The argument here is that the departure from gold gave plausibility and purchase to arguments about the 'national economy'. It did not preordain the success of Keynesian conceptions, whose success was predicated on other factors, to be discussed below. But, without this departure (which was of course *forced* on the authorities), monetary, fiscal or any other policies aimed at regulating the national economy would not have gained even as much ground as they did.

II

A policy of manipulating the budget to affect the level of output and employment is clearly predicated on a budget of sufficient size relative to other economic magnitudes, in order that budget changes will have significant consequences for the economy as a whole. For Keynesian policy, therefore, large-scale government expenditure is a *sine qua non*. In addition an effective budgetary policy requires that government revenues and expenditures be sufficiently under the control of the central authorities so that the effects of national budgetary policy are not offset by other, local and regional, authorities (as happened in the USA in the 1930s[19] where Federal deficits were offset by non-Federal surpluses). Equally the constituents of the budget must be open to manipulation sufficiently easily to allow them to be varied to pursue policies to change the level of output and employment.

In Britain the first condition, a large total government budget, was increasingly satisfied in the relevant period up to the end of the Second World War. From 14.4 per cent of GNP in 1900, total government expenditure fell (after the Boer War) to 12.8 per cent in 1910, rose again to over 50 per cent in the First World War, and then fell back to around 25 per cent. From the mid-1930s the figure rose again reaching approximately 75 per cent during the Second World War, falling back thereafter to 35-45 per cent in the post-war decade.[20]

Why did expenditure grow in this way? As always in the social sciences there are what purport to be general theories in this case of government expenditure growth – the best known being that of Adolph Wagner.[21] Writing in late nineteenth-century Germany he argued that, in industrializing countries with a rising per capita income, public expenditure would inevitably increase because of, *inter alia*, the need for co-ordination and administration of an increasingly complex society, the need efficiently to manage large investments, and the need to bring about economic stability.

Whether this really should be conceived of as a *general* theory seems open to doubt, given its specific nature.[22] In any case the argument depends on a crude teleology – public expenditure growth is inevitable. This was linked to the prescriptive character of Wagner's formulations – increasing expenditure was what the state ought to do. Finally the argument implies that, broadly, the state reacts to demands upon it and that there are no clear constraints on the revenue-raising side. All these elements mean that Wagner's theory is not a very useful basis for explaining the rise in twentieth-century British public expenditure.

A more specific argument has been put by Peacock and Wiseman.[23] It does not completely rely on, but does place heavy emphasis on a displacement effect whereby the tolerable burden of taxation is changed and this changes the amount of expenditure which can be financed. If war, revolution and depression are the three horsemen of the tax apocalypse, the emphasis of Peacock and Wiseman is very much on the first of these. It is above all in wartime that large-scale social disturbances occur which shift the boundaries of the tolerable bounds of taxation. The emphasis on the displacement effect of major wars in bringing major upward shifts in British public expenditure raised a number of problems. First is the assumption that government expenditure is always pressing against the bounds set by taxation, so that the emphasis is on those factors which affect tax levels rather than those which directly affect expenditure. Their view of expenditure is similar to the 'economics of politics' approach criticized in the introduction. Secondly the notion of a 'tolerable burden of taxation' is not really developed and it is not clear how it should be defined. For example, if tax rates are progressive, the receipts are all spent, and GNP per head is increasing, then government expenditure as a share of GNP will rise without any 'displacement effect' being needed.[24] Thirdly and more empirically, Peacock and Wiseman's own evidence does not clearly show a permanent displacement effect. The chart on p.57 of their book seems consistent with the argument that whilst wars shift public expenditure up, this after a while falls away and the rising trend already in existence continues on the same interrupted path, rather than on a new higher level.

These points are made to stress the dubious nature of any general conceptions of public expenditure growth. The argument of this chapter is not dependent on any such conception. The causes of the growth in public expenditure are only relevant in the sense of making the point that this growth can in no way be conceived of as the effect of any economic theory. Equally the effect of public expenditure growth does not have to be given any general effect, unlike for example in the 'economics of politics' conceptions where such growth is seen as a departure from the operations of the market mechanism. The pertinence of government expenditure growth here is highly specific – it is one of the necessary preconditions of an effective budgetary policy.

Equally important and parallel to this growth has been the change in the locus of control of this expenditure. Firstly, the twentieth century, unlike the nineteenth, has seen the growth of the share of central government in total government expenditure. Broadly, local government expenditure has grown in line with GNP since 1900, whilst total government expenditure roughly quadrupled in the first half of this century. This has been brought about by a shift in functions from local authorities to central e.g. National Insurance and National Health replacing the Poor Law and local institutions of welfare provision.[25] Like the growth in total expenditure this centralization has no single cause. One powerful factor has been that many proponents of welfare reform have seen nationwide equality of treatment as a central objective (rather than, for example, local accountability and control) and this has been thought to be only attainable by centralized authorities.

Even within the areas of expenditure still in the hands of local authorities, central finance has become increasingly important, and local rates decreasingly so. Whilst this does not necessarily lead to increasing central control, it does of course provide one of the means for such control, and has been used as such. Wiseman summarised the position so:

> during this century local authorities have been transformed from general purveyors of welfare and 'environmental services' enjoying a good deal of local discretion into providers of education, housing and some specialised welfare services, subject to much more detailed central control.[26]

By 1945, the growth of public expenditure and the changes in its composition and control had, in principle, made plausible the manipulation of the budget to affect the economy in a way inconceivable at the beginning of the 1930s. Arguments such as those put forward by the government at the end of the 1920s against public works expenditure proposals would have been much less cogent at the end of the Second World War. But, paradoxically perhaps, post-war budgetary policy has not been largely a case of changing government expenditures. Even with the changes detailed above, governments from 1945 onwards, certainly up to the mid-1960s, have relied predominantly on variations in tax levels to adjust the budget: revenue has proved much more easy to manipulate than expenditure.

The reasons for concentration on the revenue side in fiscal policy are several-fold, some highly conjunctural (see below Section IV) others more permanent. Amongst the latter are the constraints imposed by the annual budget system. Most of the decisions on expenditure were and are necessarily taken over a long period of time and by the time a budget is to be prepared, a few months before the new fiscal year begins, much of this expenditure is committed. This is not an 'irrationality': the period required for planning and implementing most forms of expenditure was and is an unavoidably prolonged one, with only a few items like subsidies and transfer payment levels amenable to changes in the short run. In the sphere of public investment, where so much of the argument ranged in the inter-war period, central government's ability to control is fairly restricted. In this period, nationalized industries and other public investing authorities had considerable autonomy from government control and so could not be readily made to adjust investment spending to fit in with fiscal policy.[27] Also, whilst governments could alter the rates of transfer payments, actual expenditure on these was 'demand-determined' – the total expenditure would depend on the take-up rate which could never be known with precision in advance.

This kind of adjustment in taxation required that tax revenue be substantial, amenable to central regulation, and of such a form that fairly rapid adjustments would be possible, so that the central government could bring about significant and effective tax changes in a relatively short time. All these requirements were to a large degree met by 1945. Total revenue rose in line with expenditure. Most of this accrued to the central government – local authority rates, though often acrimoniously debated, were never a substantial element in total taxation. Within the total of central taxation there was a sharp shift to direct taxation during the Second World War, its share rising to 63 per cent in 1945.[28] The wartime expansion of direct taxation necessarily meant an extension of income tax down the income scale, which meant that changes in the tax would have generalized effects on the economy. A by-product of the extension of income taxation was the general institution of a system of weekly and monthly deductions in 1940, which in 1943 led to the 'Pay As You Earn' system (PAYE). This came about to make possible the taxation of relatively low income earners who would have had problems with the previous system of bi-annual payments. PAYE meant that tax changes could be rapidly transmitted to affect the level of expenditure in the economy.[29]

By the end of the Second World War a budgetary system which made possible annual effective adjustments had come into being. Of course this was by no means a system, on either side of the account, where central government faced no constraints. Local authorities still had revenue-raising powers and considerable room for manoeuvre on expenditure levels, as did nationalized industries. Many elements of the accounts could be changed only in the face of severe political and administrative difficulties, though in the early post-war period these were not as important as they were in the 1970s because the scale of budgetary adjustment needed was small as a result of the buoyancy of the economy. However, the overall position in 1945 was very different from that of fifteen years earlier. In 1930 an effective fiscal policy would have been impossible because of the scale and structure of government finance. By 1945, within certain parameters, the means had been provided.

III

A further pre-requisite for a fiscal policy, in the sense given above, is an elaborated system of national accounts. Only with these can the likely effect of budgetary changes on the economy of the nation be assessed.

National Accounts of one kind or another have a very long history, dating back in England at least to Petty and, some would maintain, earlier than that.[30] The objectives of such accounting varied over time. In Britain in the late nineteenth century and early twentieth century, attempts, such as Bowley's, were commonly aimed at quantifying social problems – part of the concern with poverty discussed in Chapter 1.[31] Flux's estimate of National Income in 1924 was more overtly political, part of an attempt to show that 'restriction of productive effort is not the direct road to increased general welfare, as is proclaimed by some modern prophets and has been preached by earlier doctrinaires'.[32] In Britain National Income accounting was not, until Colin Clark's work, linked to business cycle theory, but was essentially Marshallian in the sense of attempting to 'quantify economic choices' within a static framework.[33]

In America the pattern of development was very different.[34] Particularly after the foundation of the National Bureau of Economic Research (NBER) in 1920 much more elaborate estimates of US National Income were prepared. Others came from the Brookings Institution and the National Industrial Conference Board (founded 1916). These efforts dwarfed the development in Britain which was largely carried out by individuals until the foundation of the National Institute for Economic and Social Research (NIESR) in 1938. Also state agencies in the USA became involved much earlier than in Britain. The Federal Trade Commission published some estimates in 1926, but more importantly the Department of Commerce took up the National Bureau estimates early in the 1930s and began to develop and publish a continuing series of estimates. In the 1930s a variety of agencies, public and private, were publishing National Income accounts for the USA. Particularly important were the efforts of Kuznets, Warburton and Currie and associates, at the National Bureau and Department of Commerce, Brookings and the Federal Reserve respectively. As in Britain the earlier stress on income distribution became secondary and the work was linked to business cycles and the depression.

For the concerns of this chapter it is important to question how far these different developments were linked to Keynesian theory. First at a general level it is clear that the elaborate work in the USA began wholly independently of Keynesian theory. As Carson notes of the USA in the 1930s, 'estimation of the output of commodities and services progressed along three main lines, all three of which were independent of Keynesian thinking at the time the studies were begun'.[35] A similar point is made by Patinkin: 'it is obvious that the statistical revolution as represented by Clark and Kuznet's national income estimates preceded the "Keynesian Revolution" as represented by the *General Theory*'.[36]

Secondly, even today most methods of National Income accounting are based as much on neoclassical as on Keynesian conceptions of the economy. Thus they involve conceptions of factor cost, with income flows conceptualized as rewards to factors. They also involve the notions of market prices as measures of both value to the consumer and production cost.[37] Illustrative of the 'pre-Keynesian' character of the basis of National Income accounting is the fact that all three methods of such accounting currently in use – income, output, and expenditure methods – pre-date the Keynesian revolution, albeit in crude form. In Britain up to the 1930s most estimates were based on income data, but Flux in his studies used the output method (using Census of Production data) and Feaveryear in 1931[38] pioneered estimates based on estimates of expenditure. These various methods were all of course heavily dependent on the availability of data, which meant that what was calculated commonly fell short of what was theoretically deemed desirable.

It could well be argued that what was specifically Keynesian about National Income accounting is not calculations of National Income as such but such calculations 'in relation to other economic flows, such as consumers' expenditure, government revenue and expenditure, asset formation, savings and the balance of payments'.[39] In Britain at least, on the grounds of a simple argument from chronology, it could be said that these kinds of calculations had to await the Keynesian Revolution. As Stone points out, such estimates for Britain do not appear until 1938, in Clark's *National Income and Outlay*, that is after the publication of the *General Theory*. However in the USA even such a chronological argument is difficult to sustain because, right from the beginning of the New Deal, Currie and Krost at the Federal Reserve were preparing estimates on the lines suggested by Stone.

They calculated

> the government's 'net contribution' to disposable income ... by making adjustments in the Federal expenditure and revenue figures. In order to estimate the 'income-creating' effects of the net contribution thus computed, it was necessary to relate it to current estimates of National Income, savings and business investment. These statistical analyses aimed at measuring the effect of fiscal policy on consumer incomes and expenditure and on business investment.[40]

Thus part of the enormous florescence of US National Income accounting in the early 1930s produced estimates in a form which in Britain only came several years later.

The terms on which National Income accounting became part of official government budgeting in 1941 is also instructive. Keynes was personally very important to this through his publications such as *How to Pay for the War* and his encouragement of Stone and others to do the work which resulted in the first official figures integrating the government budget and national income estimates.[41] The official acceptance of such calculations was based on the particular circumstances faced by the government, especially the Treasury, from early in the war. It represented not a theoretical conversion to Keynesianism but the taking up of certain forms of accounting to aid in the objectives which the Treasury conceived of as central – stopping inflation and limiting the National Debt. Initially the latter objective predominated but soon after the war began it became apparent that, because of the war-time index-linking of wages, price rises would not limit consumption, so the Treasury became even more strongly anti-inflation. Keynes's concern was above all with inflation because of its distributive effects, and so these separate paths converged.[42]

Thus 'Keynesian' accounting procedures were adopted for very specific reasons – nothing to do with unemployment for example, which was by this time no longer a problem. The use of such procedures in relation to employment was thus not inscribed in their adoption – that developed out of the particular circumstances towards the end of the war (see below). An interesting commentary on the status of such methods is given by the reaction of Robbins and Hayek. They had been perhaps the most vociferous critics of theoretical Keynesianism in the 1930s, yet they were enthusiastic supporters of Keynes's *How to Pay for the War*. Hayek wrote to Keynes,[43] 'I find myself in practically complete agreement insofar as policy during the war is concerned. It is reassuring that we agree so completely on the economics of scarcity, even if we differ on when it applies.' For Hayek, such proposals were not theoretically unpalatable, and their objective – the prevention of inflation – he obviously endorsed. Hayek's endorsement well illustrates the non-revolutionary character of these proposals.

To summarize the argument of this section: Keynes's *personal* involvement in the development of National Income accounting in Britain has contributed to an exaggeration of the importance of Keynesian theory to such accounting. Most of what occurred was not dependent on Keynesian theory, and though, once in existence, Keynesian theory did interact with National Income accounting, it is perfectly plausible to argue that the role of such theory was far from vital in forging the means of assessing the effects of budgetary policy on the economy as a whole.

IV

As argued in Chapter 4 unemployment had become an object of economic policy before the Keynesian revolution. In that sense Keynesian arguments did not create a new terrain but took place on one already in existence. The emergence of *full* employment as an articulated goal of economic policy came after the Keynesian revolution in theory, but cannot be seen as simply the effect of that revolution. What Stein says of the US is also true of Britain:[44] 'The eminence of the full employment goal arose out of a particular historical situation and would be affected by subsequent historical developments.'

The emergence of full employment as a goal for British policy at the end of the Second World War can very broadly be linked to two features of that war. Firstly the nature of the war as a 'total war', involving in active pursuit of war objectives the great bulk of the population, meant that popular support for the war was vital to its successful prosecution. Titmuss has made this point in respect of social policy during the war. Strategists were convinced that 'the war could not be won unless millions of ordinary people, in Britain and overseas, were convinced that we had something better to offer than had our enemies – not only during but after the war'.[45] Partly because of this, plans for social change were produced whilst the war was still at its height – above all of course the Beveridge Report on Social Insurance in 1942. Whilst unemployment by this time might be seen as strictly an economic problem, the Beveridge Report made clear that its proposals depended upon the government maintaining full employment after the war.

The euphoric popular reception of the Beveridge Report[46] reflected another facet of change during the war – the radicalization of the population. Whatever the multiple causes of this change[47] it meant that the strategy of social reform as part of fighting the war was realistic in the sense of reflecting popular political feeling. Thus a strong reformist politics became a pre-condition for electoral success, and the Conservatives, both because of their own internal structure and because of their association with all the problems of the 1930s, became the losers in 1945. However, the triumph of Labour in 1945 should not mask the fact that much of their legislative programme was mooted in the war period. Their position was one, as it were, of legatees of a position in the creation of which they played only a small part.

This radicalization of the population meant that full employment could be seen not only as a necessary adjunct to social reform but also as an important goal in its own right. Bevin recounted how he and Churchill, saying farewell to troops just before D-Day 1944, had constantly encountered the question 'Ernie, when we have done this job for you are we going back on the dole?' Both he and Churchill replied 'No, you are not'. As Addison suggests, 'Apart from housing, the employment issue was the one that mattered most to ordinary people'.[48]

Under these circumstances, talk of full employment existed from the early war years. Much of this was linked not to fiscal policy at all but to socialist arguments about state control of production and to detailed planning of the deployment of labour – conceptions which Beveridge in his report depended upon.[49] Official work on full employment was being carried out by Meade and others from 1941 in the Economic Section of the War Cabinet. Eventually of course this and similar work gave birth to the White Paper on Employment Policy of 1944 (spurred on to publication by the knowledge that Beveridge was preparing his own unofficial document on full employment, which in fact appeared a few months after the White Paper).

Perhaps only the first sentence of the White Paper was

unambiguous: 'The Government accept as one of their primary aims and responsibilities the maintenance of a high and stable level of employment after the war.'[50] Its proposals on budgetary policy for controlling the level of employment were tentative. Stress was laid on varying social insurance contributions and local government investment, neither of which ideas came to be used. Also one paragraph of the White Paper stressed the need after the war for a 'budgetary equilibrium such as will maintain the confidence in the future which is necessary for a healthy and enterprising industry'.

Overall it would not be much exaggerated to say that except as a sign of their conception of political realities which led the authorities to the full employment commitment, the White Paper should not be seen as of great importance. The mechanisms of post-war budgetary policy owed most to the exigencies outlined in Section III above plus other conjunctural features of the war and post-war economy. Firstly, the pattern of tax rather than expenditure adjustment was strongly established during the war period. Expenditure on the war was seen as largely fixed by non-financial concerns, and then tax adjusted to this as far as possible. Secondly, the pre-war stress on expenditure as the basis for fiscal policy depended upon a conception of a long-term if not permanent tendency to stagnation and unemployment. A fiscal policy to remedy this did not require great flexibility. The post-1945 problem was of course different, it was to adjust policy around full employment, so that flexibility was central.

If Matthews' argument, quoted at the beginning of this chapter, is accepted then the relation between the governmental commitment to full employment and the 'fact' of full employment can be reformulated. Rather than the commitment leading to the 'fact', the relation was more the reverse. Because non-governmental factors (high private investment, booming world trade, etc.) maintained near-full employment then the 'commitment' could be sustained without too much difficulty. Full employment as an object of policy making only becomes problematic when the conditions of its realization change, and fiscal policy can no longer be carried on in the context of a generally buoyant economy. Full employment did not largely arise from changes in economic theory; equally its demise was not conditioned mainly by theoretical changes, but by changes in the *means* necessary for its realization.

Notes

Place of publication is London unless otherwise indicated.

Introduction

1 G.K. Shaw, *An Introduction to the Theory of Macro-Economic Policy*, 3rd edn, 1977, Introduction.

2 For the twentieth century see particularly S. Howson, *Domestic Monetary Management in Britain 1919-38*, Cambridge, 1975; S. Howson and D. Winch, *The Economic Advisory Council 1930–39*, Cambridge, 1977; D. Winch, *Economics and Policy*, 1969.

3 For earlier periods see, for example, C. Wilson, 'Government policy and private interest in modern Economic History' in *Economic History and the Historian*, 1969; A.J. Taylor, *State Intervention and Laissez-Faire*, 1972, especially Chapter 4.

4 J.M. Keynes, *The General Theory of Employment, Interest and Money. Collected Writings* vol. VII, 1973, p.383.

5 R. Skidelsky, 'The reception of the Keynesian Revolution' in M. Keynes (ed.), *Essays on John Maynard Keynes*, Cambridge, 1975, argues that this was not Keynes's own position.

6 Winch, op. cit., pp.24-5.

7 Howson and Winch, op. cit.

8 T.W. Hutchinson, *Economics and Economic Policy in Britain 1946-66*, 1968, Appendix.

9 Howson and Winch, op. cit., p.164.

10 Howson, op. cit., p.1.

11 E. Mandel, *Late Capitalism*, 1975, p.481.

12 B. Hindess, 'The concept of class in Marxist theory and Marxist politics' in J. Bloomfield (ed.), *Class Hegemony and Party*, 1977.

13 A. Gamble and P. Walton, *Capitalism in Crisis*, 1976, p.33.

14 S. Pollard (ed.), *The Gold Standard and Employment Politics Between the Wars*, 1970, Introduction.

15 Though see E.G. West, 'Educational slowdown and public intervention in nineteenth-century England', *Explorations in Economic History*, 12(1), 1975.

16 L. Robbins, *The Nature and Significance of Economic Science*, 1932, p.16.

17 G. Becker, *The Economic Approach to Human Behaviour*, Chicago, 1976, Introduction.

18 A. Downs, *An Economic Theory of Democracy*, New York, 1957.

19 W.A. Niskamen, *Bureaucracy: Servant or Master?*, Hobart Paperback 5, IEA, 1973.

20 For example, G. Stigler, 'The theory of economic regulation', *Bell Journal*, 3, 1971.

21 For example, S. Brittan, 'Inflation and democracy' in F. Hirsch and J. Goldthorpe (eds), *The Political Economy of Inflation*, 1978.

22 J.M. Buchanan *et al.*, *The Consequences of Mr. Keynes*, Hobart Paper 78, IEA, 1978.

23 G. Tullock, *The Vote Motive*, Hobart Paperback 9, IEA, 1976, p.29.

24 Buchanan *et al.*, op. cit., p.17.

25 For an application of this to modern inflation and policy see R.J. Gordon, 'The demand for and supply of inflation', *Journal of Law and Economics*, vol. 18, no. 3, 1975.

26 G. Stigler, 'Do economists matter?, *Southern Economic Journal*, vol. 42, no. 3, 1976.

27 G. Thompson, 'Capitalist Profit Calculation and Inflation Accounting', *Economy and Society*, vol. 7, no. 4, 1978.

28 But see M. Jensen and W. Meckling, 'Theory of the firm: managerial behaviour, agency costs and ownership structure', *Journal of Financial Economics*, vol. 3, no. 4, 1976.

29 Tullock, op. cit., pp. 36–40.

30 P.Q. Hirst, 'Althusser and the Theory of Ideology', *Economy and Society*, vol. 5, no. 4, 1978, pp. 407–11.

31 H.F. Pitkin, *The Concept of Representation*, Berkeley, 1967.

32 This raises the question of the relationship to 'Institutionalist Economics' – Veblen, Commons, Mitchell, etc. Overall this book shares with them only a critical view of orthodox economics and a belief in the importance of institutions. Institutionalist Economics is made up of a highly heterogeneous set of texts, with little but these negative features in common. Its most explicit theorist, Commons, develops a sophisticated conception of institutions, but one which depends on very problematic concepts like 'scarcity' and 'purpose'. See J.R. Commons, *Legal Foundations of Capitalism*, 1924 and *Institutional Economics*, 1934.

Chapter 1

1 W. Beveridge, *Unemployment: A Problem of Industry*, 1909, p.4.

2 W. Beveridge, *Full Employment in a Free Society*, 1944, pp.40–6 and pp.328–37.

3 See Beveridge, *Unemployment*, op. cit., pp.16–23 and (Balfour) Committee on Trade and Industry, *Survey of Industrial Relations*, 1928.

4 Figures for these groups back to 1851 are published in the second series of *Memoranda, Statistical Tables and Charts on British and Foreign Trade and Industry*, Cd. 2317, Parliamentary Papers, 1905, LXXXIV.

5 Beveridge, *Unemployment*, op. cit., pp.1–2 assumes that the emergence of unemployment as a problem for policy parallels its appearance in fact, but offers no evidence.

6 G. Stedman Jones, *Outcast London*, Oxford, 1971. In discussing this book I have learnt a great deal from the excellent review article by K. Williams, 'Problematic History', *Economy and Society*, vol. I, no. 4, 1972.

7 Stedman Jones, op. cit., p.v.

8 ibid., p.286.

9 Unemployment figures were first published in the 1880s by the Board of Trade based on Trade Union figures, thus giving official recognition to the largely artisan unemployed.

10 Stedman Jones, op. cit., pp.287–8, 327.

11 ibid., pp.36–7 and 56–7.

12 For a critique of such conceptions see B. Hindess, *Philosophy and Methodology in the Social Sciences*, Brighton, 1977, especially Chapter 7.

13 Stedman Jones, op. cit., p.336.

14 ibid., pp.268 and 300–1.

15 A text which covers similar ground to *Outcast London* but generally avoids epistemological criteria is J. Harris, *Unemployment and Politics: A Study in English Social Policy 1886–1914*, Oxford, 1972.

16 Williams, op. cit., p.466.

17 R.C.O. Matthews, 'Why has Britain had full employment since the war?', *Economic Journal*, 78, 1968, p.565.

18 *Majority Report*, Part VI, Chapter 1, paras. 167–201. *Minority Report*, Conclusion, Chapter 4.

19 On the basis of extreme dubious evidence, i.e. Sidney Webb's evidence that the number of general labourers in the 1891 census greatly exceeded the number in 1851. Royal Commission on Poor Laws, *Appendix, Vol. IX, Evidence Relating to Unemployment*, Cd. 5068, Parliamentary Papers, 1910, XLIX, Q93199 and S. Webb, *Memorandum*.

20 J. Harris: *William Beveridge: A Biography*, Oxford, 1977, Chapters 6 and 7.

21 Royal Commission on Poor Laws, *Replies of Distress Committees to Questions Circulated on the Subject of the Unemployed Workmen Act 1905*, Cd.4499 Parliamentary Papers, 1909, XLV, p. 1.

22 E.g. Royal Commission on Poor Laws, *Effects of Employment or Assistance given to the 'Unemployed' since 1886 as a means of Relieving Distress Outside the Poor Law*, Cd.4795 Parliamentary Papers, 1909, XLIV, Q4795.

23 Harris, *Unemployment and Politics*, op. cit., p.161. Booth, *Life and Labour of the People in London*, 1st series 1902, I, p.33.

24 J. Brown: 'Charles Booth and labour colonies', *Economic History Review*, vol. XXI, no. 2, 1968, p.353.

25 Booth, op. cit., I, p.162 and p.176. Class B are described as 'casual earnings, very poor'.

26 ibid., pp.165–9, and J. Brown, op. cit.

27 Cds. 2175, 2210, 2186, Parliamentary Papers, XXXII, 1904.

28 The title of a book by G.R. Searle, Oxford, 1971. See also N. Rose, 'The Psychological Complex: Mental Measurement and Social Administration', *Ideology and Consciousness*, no. 5, 1979, pp.5–68.

29 ibid., pp.1–2.

30 On eugenics see B. Semmel, *Imperialism and Social Reform*, 1960, pp.45–52.

31 Searle, *The Quest for National Efficiency*, op. cit., pp.67–71, and Chapter VII.

32 Booth, op. cit., I, pp.166–7, J. Brown, op. cit., p.354.

33 Stedman Jones, op. cit., p.335.

34 Beveridge, *Unemployment*, op. cit.

35 ibid., p.201.

36 ibid., p.233. See also Harris, *William Beveridge*, op. cit., Ch. 6, esp. p.119.

37 ibid., p.3.

38 D. Winch, *Economics and Policy*, 1969, pp.52–7.

39 Beveridge, *Unemployment*, op. cit., p.134.

40 Williams, op. cit., p.464. Of course concern with 'individual character' has not been absent from discussion of unemployment in the 1970s and beginning of the 1980s. There is no reason why unemployment should remain an 'economic' problem in the way it has predominantly been in the post 1945 period.

41 Harris, *Unemployment and Politics*, op. cit., p.6.

42 A Cutler, 'The romance of labour', *Economy and Society*, vol. 7, no. 1, 1978, p.92.

43 Harris, *Unemployment and Politics*, Chapter 6 and p.356.

44 This tends to be the position of Winch, op. cit., pp.52–64.

Chapter 2

1 *1st Interim Report of the Committee on Currency and Foreign Exchanges After the War*, Cd. 9182, Parliamentary Papers 1918, VII, para. 47.

2 R.S. Sayers, *Bank of England Operations, 1890–1914*, 1936.

3 The notion of a 'real' economy begs many questions. It is difficult to justify either as a simple opposition to the monetary – why is money not

'real'? – or as an appeal to epistemological principle, where the assertion of the 'reality' of something merely functions to give one conception an uncontested privilege over another.

4 E.J. Hobsbawm, *Industry and Empire*, 1968, p.200.

5 M. de Cecco, *Money and Empire*, Oxford, 1974, Chapter 3. See also A. Ford, *The Gold Standard 1880–1914: Britain and Argentina*, Oxford, 1962.

6 F.W. Fetter, *The Development of British Monetary Orthodoxy*, Harvard, 1965, p.2.

7 ibid., Chapter 3.

8 E.g. W. Rees-Mogg, *The Reigning Error*, 1974.

9 Fetter, op. cit., p.143.

10 ibid.

11 ibid., pp.74–6.

12 ibid., pp.102–3.

13 de Cecco, op. cit., p.41. Portugal went on to the standard in 1854.

14 Ford, op. cit., p.133.

15 As Malcolm Falkus has pointed out to me this was partly because by normal criteria the pound was undervalued substantially at $4.86, a point rather lost in subsequent discussion of that rate after the First World War.

16 Royal Commission on Recent Changes in the Relative Values of the Precious Metals, *Final Report*, C.5512, Parliamentary Papers, 1888, XLV.

17 For Europe the same contrast is apparent – see B.R. Mitchell, *European Historical Statistics 1758–1978*, 1975, Table C.1.

18 P.J. Perry, *British Agriculture 1875–1914*, 1973, p.xxvi, and G. Kitson Clark, *The Making of Victorian England*, 1962, p.216.

19 Perry, op. cit., p.xxxiv.

20 W. Ashworth, *An Economic History of England 1870–1939*, 1960, p.200.

21 P.H. Lindert, *Key Currencies and Gold 1900–30*, Princeton, 1969, p.2.

22 J.H. Clapham, *The Bank of England: A History*, Cambridge, 1944, vol. II, p.382.

23 R.S. Sayers, *The Bank of England 1891–1944*, Cambridge, 1976, vol. I, p.29.

24 At a press conference in Washington on 3 December 1965 the following exchange took place: Reporter: 'why do you have balance of payments problems now when you didn't have them 50 years ago?' James Callaghan: 'There were no balance of payments problems 50 years ago because there were no balance of payments statistics.' Quoted in Lindert, op. cit., p.36. On balance of payments statistics see M.D.K.W. Foot, 'The Balance of Payments in the Inter-War Period', *Bank of England Quarterly Bulletin*, vol. 12, no. 3, September 1972.

25 P. Deane and W.A. Cole, *British Economic Growth 1688–1959*, Cambridge, 1962, p.36.

26 A.H. Imlah, *Economic Elements in the Pax Britannica*, Harvard, 1958, p.191.

27 V. Smith, *The Rationale of Central Banking*, 1936, p.2.

28 W. Bagehot, *Lombard Street*, 1873.

29 Smith, op. cit., p.3 and pp.21–3.

30 J. Viner, 'Clapham on the Bank of England', *Economica*, XIII, no. 46, 1945, pp.61–2.

31 Clapham, op. cit., II, p.274. See also J. Morley, *Life of Gladstone* (1903), vol. I, p.650.

32 Sayers, *Bank of England Operations* op. cit., p.135.

33 ibid., p.125.

34 R.S. Sayers, *Central Banking after Bagehot*, Oxford, 1957, p.11.

35 ibid., p.13.

36 Cf. W.M. Scammell, *The London Discount Market*, 1968, p.185.

37 Sayers, *Bank of England Operations*, op. cit., p.127.

38 Scammell, op. cit., p.170.

39 W.T.C. King, *History of the London Discount Market*, 1936, p.269.

40 Committee on Finance and Industry, *Report*, CMD. 3899, para. 295.

41 Ford, op. cit., p.181, see also Lindert, op. cit., pp.56-7.

42 Lindert, op. cit., pp.33–5.

43 ibid., p.17.

44 de Cecco, op. cit., p.62.

45 ibid., Appendix A.

46 On this issue see J.M. Keynes, *Indian Currency and Finance*, 1913 (*Collected Writings* vol. I), Chapter 6. Keynes points out that even if gold is held in India this by no means implies that it cannot be attracted into London under certain circumstances. See also de Cecco, op. cit., Chapter 4.

47 de Cecco, op. cit., p.105.

48 Clapham, op. cit., vol. I, p.225.

49 de Cecco, op. cit., especially Chapter 6.

50 ibid., p.105.

51 Keynes, op. cit., Chapter 2.

52 de Cecco, op. cit., pp.118–26.

53 Sayers, *Bank of England Operations*, op. cit., p.104.

54 Based on H. Withers, *The Meaning of Money*, 2nd edn, 1909, p.102.

Chapter 3

1 A. Cutler, B. Hindess, P. Hirst, A. Hussain, *Marx's Capital and Capitalism Today*, 1978, vol. II, p.3.

2 W.L. Strauss, *Joseph Chamberlain and the Theory of Imperialism*, Washington, 1942, p.96.

3 A.W. Coats (ed.), *The Classical Economists and Economic Policy*, 1971, p.28.

4 L. Brown, *The Board of Trade and the Free Trade Movement*, 1830-42, Oxford, 1958, p.2.

5 See N. McCord, *The Anti-Corn Law League*, 1958 and G. Kitson Clark, 'The repeal of the Corn Laws and the politics of the forties', *Economic History Review*, IV, 1 January 1951.

6 Thus for example Cobden's remark that 'three weeks of showery weather, when the wheat is in bloom, would repeal the Corn Laws'. Quoted in S. Buxton, *Finance and Politics: An Historical Study 1783–1885*, 1888, vol. I, p.79.

7 H. Roseveare, *The Treasury*, 1969, p.143.

8 ibid., p.187.

9 J. Clapham, *The Bank of England: A History*, Cambridge, 1944, vol. II, pp.272–4.

10 H. Llewellyn Smith, *The Board of Trade*, 1928, p.57.

11 Roseveare, op. cit., p.187.

12 Buxton, op. cit., p.135.

13 A. Peacock and J. Wiseman, *The Growth of Public Expenditure in the United Kingdom*, 1967, p.35.

14 Buxton, op. cit., p.319.

15 E. Halevy, *Imperialism and the Rise of Labour*, 1961, p.315. Cobdenite economists advocated the complete reliance on direct taxes, indirect taxes being seen as logically at variance with free trade. See, for example, T.E.C. Leslie, *Financial Reform*, Cobden Club Essays, 1871.

16 Roseveare, op. cit., p.191.

17 Not, of course, that these had ever entirely disappeared – see, for example, A Manchester Man (R. Burn), *An Inquiry into the Commercial Position of Great Britain and the Causes of the Present Ruinous and Alarming State of our Manufacturing Industries*, Manchester, 1869.

18 B.H. Brown, *The Tariff Reform Movement in Great Britain 1881-1895*, Columbia, 1943, p.139.

19 C.J. Fuchs, *The Trade Policy of Britain and her Colonies since 1860*, 1905, p.178. Also A.J. Balfour, *Economic Notes on Insular Free Trade and Speech at Sheffield*, 1903, p.23.

20 'A law which prevents the people of England from buying in France or America is in no essential respect different from a law which prevents the people of Middlesex from buying in Surrey or Lancashire.' T.H. Farrer, *Free Trade versus Fair Trade*, 1885, p.1.

21 'The historical political economy of the present day ... must repudiate English Free Trade, which, by its uncompromising insistence on

international division of labour, implies ultimately a denial of the independent national economy', C.J. Fuchs, op. cit., p.xxv.

22 'English trade and foreign competition', *Quarterly Review*, vol. 152, no. 303, July 1881.

23 R. Giffen, 'The use of import and export statistics' in his *Economic Inquiries and Studies*, 1904, vol. I. Originally published in 1882.

24 C4893, Parliamentary Papers, vol. XXIII, 1886.

25 'Fair Trade and British Labour', *Quarterly Review*, vol. 152, no. 304, October 1881, p.555. See also B. Semmel, *Imperialism and Social Reform*, 1960, p.200.

26 E.E. Williams, *Made in Germany*, 1896, reprinted Brighton, 1973, pp.4–5.

27 A.R. Ilersic and P.F.B. Leddle, *Parliament of Commerce: The Story of the Association of British Chambers of Commerce 1896–1960*, 1960, p.30. Also T.H. Farrer, *The State in its Relation to Trade*, 1883, p.9.

28 Free Traders were not always consistent in their response. Giffen gave what is usually considered the orthodox view when he discounted the possibility of general unemployment because wage changes would counteract this. See his 'The present economic conditions and outlook for the United Kingdom' in *Economic Inquiries and Essays*, op. cit., p.412. D. Hunter in *Tariffs and Unemployment*, 1910 argued that tariffs were no remedy for unemployment, as the latter existed in all countries with or without tariffs.

29 S.H. Zebel, 'Fair Trade: an English reaction to the breakdown of the Cobden Treaty System', *Journal of Modern History*, XII, 2 June 1940.

30 J. Amery, *Life of Joseph Chamberlain*, 1969, vol. 5, p.356.

31 W.A.S. Hewins, *The Apologia of an Imperialist*, 1929, vol. I, p.234.

32 Lord Brassey, *Sixty Years of Progress: and the New Fiscal Policy*, 1906; J. Chamberlain, *Tariff Reform and the Agricultural Industry*, Birmingham, 1904.

33 Semmel, op. cit., pp.150-3.

34 Amery, op. cit., vol. V, p.267; Chamberlain, *Tariff Reform and the Agricultural Industry*, op. cit., p.11.

35 Charles Booth, in *Fiscal Reform*, No. 251, January 1904, p.699.

36 Balfour, op. cit., p.5.

37 J. Chamberlain, *Tariff Reform and the Colonial Conference*, Birmingham, 1904, p.9; see also C.W. Boyd (ed.), *Mr Chamberlain's Speeches*, 1914, vol. II, p.267. Here Holland was used as an example of the kind of economy which England under free trade threatened to become.

38 Though see the quotation from a fair trade tract cited in T.H. Farrer, *Free Trade versus Fair Trade*, 1885, p.108.

39 This would not have been a problem in respect to the Empire because most British foreign investment was not in the Empire. See, for example,

M. Simon, 'The pattern of new British portfolio foreign investment, 1865–1914', in A.R. Hall (ed.), *The Export of Capital from Britain 1870–1914*, 1968, p.23.

40 For example, Brassey, op. cit., p.124.

41 See Balfour's characteristic ambiguity on foreign investment in his *Economic Notes*, op. cit., p.9, where he notes the receipt of dividends as a source of finance for imports but then suggests that foreign investment is also harmful because it lessens employment in Britain.

42 Hewins, op. cit., vol. I, p.56.

43 A. Milner, *The Nation and the Empire*, 1913, p.xxxii.

44 See, for example in the discussion, in Amery, op. cit., vol. V, pp.270–4.

45 P. Harnetty, *Imperialism and Free Trade: Lancashire and India in the Mid-Nineteenth Century*, Manchester, 1972.

46 This was argued by the India Office representative at the Imperial Conference of 1907. See, *The Great Preference Debate at the Imperial Conference 1907*, 1907. (A selection from the conference minutes.)

47 Boyd (ed.), op. cit., vol. II, pp.125–40.

48 H.J. Mackinder, *Money-Power and Man-Power*, 1906, p.23.

49 Semmel, op. cit., is the classic reference.

50 N. Rose, 'The Psychological Complex; mental measurement and social administration', *Ideology and Consciousness*, no. 5, spring 1979.

51 See Semmel, op. cit., pp.141–8.

52 Peacock and Wiseman, op. cit., p.37. As a share of GNP this expenditure was roughly constant, but it is the absolute expenditure which is important in the current context.

53 B. Mallett, *British Budgets 1887–1913*, 1913, p.171.

54 ibid., table XIV, p.493.

55 Hewins, op. cit., vol. I, p.182.

56 S.B. Saul, *Studies in British Overseas Trade*, Liverpool, 1960, especially p.41 and pp.228–9. See also his 'The Economic Significance of "Constructive Imperialism"', *Journal of Economic History*, XVII, 2, 1957.

57 Semmel, op. cit.

58 ibid., pp.150–3.

Chapter 4

1 J. Harris, *Unemployment and Politics*, Oxford, 1972.

2 G. Stedman Jones, *Outcast London*, Oxford, 1971.

3 ibid., p.v. For some general discussion of the theoretical complexities of the concept unemployment see A.K. Sen, *Employment, Technology and Development*, Oxford, 1975, Ch. 1.

4 Harris, op. cit., p.6.

5 Stedman Jones, op. cit., Introduction and Part III. Note the slackening of

concern in the 1890s (p.330) and its revival after 1900 during the 'Quest for National Efficiency'.

6 One of the criticisms that might be made of Stedman Jones is that the exclusive concern with London tends to imply the absence of widespread casual labour elsewhere. For this and other points on Stedman Jones see the important review article by Karel Williams, 'Problematic History', *Economy and Society*, vol. 1, no. 4, 1972.

7 It should perhaps be noted that much of the problem in the staples was not complete unemployment, but varying periods of short-time working. For example in 1929 there were 450,000 coal miners who worked for some period but less than the full number of shifts. *Report on the Industrial Transference Board*, CMD. 3156, 1928, Parliamentary Papers X.

8 A. Milward, *The Economic Effects of the World Wars on Britain*, 1970, p.37.

9 In accordance with W. Beveridge, *Unemployment: A Problem of Industry*, 1909 edition, p.77, casual employment is taken to mean 'short engagements' and 'want of selection'.

10 For example H.A. Mess, *Casual Labour at the Docks*, 1916.

11 ibid., p.99.

12 A. Bullock, *The Life and Times of Ernest Bevin*, 1960, vol. I, p.132.

13 Ministry of Labour, *Port Labour Inquiry Report* (Maclean), 1931, para. 50.

14 H.L. Smith, *New Survey of London Life and Labour*, 1932, vol. 2, p.401.

15 B.R. Mitchell, *Abstract of British Historical Statistics*, Cambridge, 1962, p.67.

16 Ministry of Labour, op. cit., para. 84. Dockers at this time had a minimum engagement period of half a day, though one day seems to have been normal.

17 ibid., para. 103: Beveridge's evidence to the Royal Commission on Unemployment Insurance: *Minutes of Evidence*, 1931, vol. I, pp.721–3.

18 Ministry of Labour, op. cit., para.79.

19 Smith, op. cit., vol. 2, p.391.

20 London County Council, *London Statistics 1928/29*.

21 *Unemployed Persons in Receipt of Domiciliary Poor Relief*, CMD. 3006, 1927, Parliamentary Papers XIX, table VI. Of course this figure is a function of the 'liberality' of the Guardians as well as the number of unemployed.

22 D.F. Wilson, *Dockers*, 1972, pp.67–71; Beveridge, *Unemployment* (1930 edition), p.316.

23 Ministry of Labour, op. cit., para. 22.

24 *New Survey*, vol. 2, pp.45–7, p.68.

25 ibid., vol. 2, pp.26–9; vol. 8, pp.15–18; vol. 5, pp.117–18.

26 F.G. Hanham, *Report of Inquiry into Casual Labour in the Merseyside*

Area, and D. Caradog-Jones (ed.), *Social Survey of Merseyside*, Liverpool, 1934, vol. 2.

27 The Royal Commission on Unemployment Insurance *Final Report*, CMD. 4185, 1932, Parliamentary Papers 1931–2, XIII, para. 144.

28 R.C. Davison, *The Unemployed: Old Policies and New*, 1929, p.180.

29 *Report Concerning Wages and Employment of Port Labour*, (Shaw Enquiry) CMD. 936–7, 1920, Parliamentary Papers. Also Bullock, op. cit., pp.116–33.

30 Stedman Jones, op. cit., p.327.

31 ibid., pp.10–11.

32 *New Survey*, op. cit., vol. 2, p.71, p.411.

33 Parish of Poplar Borough, *Report of Special Inquiry into the Expenditure of the Guardians*, 1922. See also P. Ryan, 'Poplarism 1894–1930, in P. Thane (ed.), *The Origins of British Social Policy*, 1978.

34 *Unemployment in East London*, Toynbee Hall, 1922.

35 Stedman Jones, op. cit., especially Chapter 16.

36 It is of interest that whilst the 1909 edition of Beveridge's *Unemployment* had five references to demoralization in the index, the 1930 part of the book had none at all.

37 Stedman Jones, op. cit., Chapter 1.

38 *New Survey*, op. cit., vol. 2, p.6. Some of the change in London is swamped by the fact that 'London' here embraces 1.65m of population in the Home Countries, ibid., Appendix, Table II.

39 P. Hall, *Industries of London since 1861*, 1962, p.121.

40 The mean size of enterprises where employers exchanged insurance books July–December 1930 was 78.6 employees for electrical engineering, 67.0 for motor vehicles, 30.5 for tailoring, 32.5 for dress and millinery. (The median size in all cases was much smaller, under 10 employees in tailoring.) The data used here undoubtedly exaggerates the size of units in tailoring and dressmaking by excluding casual workers. Data from *New Survey*, op. cit., Vol. 2, Appendix, Table I.

41 D.H. Smith, *Industries of Greater London*, 1933.

42 P. Hall, op. cit.

43 See Brinley Thomas, 'The movement of labour into South East England 1920–32', *Economica*, N.S., vol. I, no. 2, 1934, who shows very large migrations from out of London into the growing factory areas, and also the very low migration into much of the East End. (Though Dagenham became important when Ford works started there in 1931.)

44 *New Survey*, op. cit., vol. 2, p.7.

45 Cf. E.J. Hobsbawm, *Labouring Men*, 1968, especially pp.300–1.

46 Stedman Jones, op. cit., pp.348–9.

47 See P. Thompson, *Socialists, Liberals and Labour: The Struggle for London*, 1967.

48 D. Winch, *Economics and Policy*, 1969, p.83.

49 D. Moggridge, *British Monetary Policy 1924–31*, Cambridge, 1972, Ch. 3.

50 R.S. Sayers, 'The return to gold, 1925' in S. Pollard (ed.), *The Gold Standard and Employment Policies Between the Wars*, 1970.

51 Moggridge, op. cit., p.69 and p.77.

52 ibid., p.69. Five years later Norman was perhaps less self-assured than this quotation suggests he was in 1925. Under some pressure he accepted the damaging effects on employment of the 1925 return. See *Committee on Finance and Industry (Macmillan), Minutes of Evidence*, 1930–1, vol. I, especially Qs. 3492–3.

53 Beveridge, op. cit.

54 Winch, op. cit., p.54.

55 This includes domestic and agricultural workers, railway men and state employees. See B. Gilbert, *British Social Policy 1914-1939*, 1970, Ch. 2.

56 For a detailed look at Unemployment Insurance in the 1920s see A. Deacon, 'Concession and coercion: the politics of Unemployment Insurance in the 1920s' in A. Briggs and J. Saville, *Essays in Labour History 1918–1939*, 1977 and E. Briggs and A. Deacon, 'The creation of the Unemployment Assistance Board', *Policy and Politics*, vol. 2, no. 1, 1973.

57 For example Winch, op. cit., pp.104–9.

58 ibid., p.111.

59 Royal Commission on Unemployment Insurance, *Minutes of Evidence*, vol. I, p.381, para. 2, 1933.

60 West Ham, for instance, was taken over by central authorities because of extravagance in 1926. S. and B. Webb, *English Local Government: English Poor Law History*, pt. 2, vol. 2, p.926. See generally Briggs and Deacon, op. cit.

61 S. and B. Webb, op. cit., pt. 2, vol. 2, pp.896-905.

62 E.W. Bakke, *Insurance or Dole?*, New Haven, 1935, p.156.

63 Broadly, labour exchanges, the Poor Law, Labour Colonies, etc. for the casual labourer; unemployment insurance for the skilled worker subject to regular seasonal fluctuations. Despite Beveridge's hopes, labour exchanges were mainly used by skilled workers; see Harris, op. cit., Ch. VIII.

64 For example, E.E. Williams, *Made in Germany*, 1896.

65 P. Thompson, op. cit., and Stedman Jones, op. cit., Ch. 19.

66 Quoted in Gilbert, op. cit., p.84.

67 See, for Unemployment Insurance, Deacon, op. cit., for the Poor Law, S. and B. Webb, op. cit., pp.910–13.

68 See, for example, D.H. Macgregor, 'Rationalisation of industry', *Economic Journal*, vol. 37, no. 4, 1927.

69 S. Howson and D. Winch, *The Economic Advisory Council 1930–39*, Cambridge, 1977, especially conclusion. For a contemporary attack on

such views see H. Laski, *The Limitations of the Expert*, 1931.
70 S. and B. Webb, op. cit., vol. 2, pp.668–9.

Chapter 5

1 Liberal Party, *We Can Conquer Unemployment*, 1929. See also Liberal Party, *Britain's Industrial Future*, 1928, reprinted 1977.
2 *Memoranda on Certain Proposals Relating to Unemployment*, CMD. 3331, Parliamentary Papers 1928–29, XVI.
3 J.M. Keynes, *Can Lloyd George Do It?*, *Collected Writings*, vol. IX, 1971.
4 For example D. Winch, *Economics and Policy*, 1972, p.119; L. Klein, *The Keynesian Revolution*, 1966, pp.12–13.
5 For example J. Harris, *Unemployment and Politics*, Oxford, 1972, p.235.
6 See Chapter 1 above.
7 Harris, op. cit., pp.157–80.
8 *Report of the Royal Commission on the Poor Laws*, Cd. 4499 Parliamentary Papers 1909, XXXVII, vol. 3, pp.657–62.
9 ibid., p.659.
10 A.C. Pigou, *Wealth and Nations*, 1912, pp.477–86.
11 R.G. Hawtrey, *Good and Bad Trade*, 1913, pp.259–61.
12 Winch, op. cit., p.60.
13 Harris, op. cit., p.344.
14 *We Can Conquer Unemployment*, p.10.
15 Harris, op. cit., pp.343–4 and p.368. See also *Hansard (Commons)* 1909, vol. X, c906–1042. Harris is obviously correct to point out that the claim in *We Can Conquer Unemployment*, p.11, that the Tories strenuously opposed the 1909 measure is untrue, though 25 voted against the Bill rather than the 6 Harris suggests.
16 *Royal Commission on the Poor Laws Minority Report*, pp.452-65, cf. *Majority Report*, vol. I, pp.264–7.
17 K. Hancock, 'The reduction of unemployment as a problem of public policy, 1920–29' in S. Pollard (ed.), *The Gold Standard and Employment Policies Between the Wars*, 1970.
18 Unemployment Grants Committee, *1st Interim Report*, 1922, p.3.
19 UGC *Final Report*, CMD. 4354, Parliamentary Papers 1932–33, vol. XV, p.5.
20 For example A. Deacon, 'Concession and Coercion: the politics of Unemployment Insurance in the 1920s' in A. Briggs and J. Saville, *Essays in Labour History 1918–1939*, 1977. The end of the belief that a revival of world trade was in prospect as a solution to unemployment is signalled by Lloyd George's advocacy of public works similar to those in *We Can Conquer Unemployment* in *The Nations and Athenaeum* 12 April 1924.

21 See also J. Tomlinson, 'Unemployment and government policy between the Wars: a note', *Journal of Contemporary History*, 13, 1, 1978.

22 J.M. Keynes, *The Means of Prosperity* in *Collected Writings*, vol. IX, 1971.

23 *Memoranda on Certain Proposals*, op. cit.

24 Winch, op. cit., p.119.

25 ibid., p.118.

26 See Keynes's *General Theory of Employment, Interest and Money*, in *Collected Writings*, vol. VII.

27 A. Speer, *Inside the Third Reich*, 1970.

28 Inter-Departmental Committee on Unemployment: *Report on* 'We Can Conquer Unemployment' *and the Melchett-Tillett Report*, Public Record Office, CAB 24/203 C.P. 104(29). Hopkins before the Macmillan Committee (*Committee on Finance and Industry, Minutes of Evidence*, 1931, vol. II, 30th day, Q5576) said that the White Paper was the 'views of officials' though this was not of course stated in the White Paper itself.

29 U.K. Hicks, *The Finance of British Government 1920–36*, 1938, reprinted 1970, p.202 and p.224.

30 For example even in London in 1929 the unemployment rate was 4.7 per cent, the lowest figure being 3.8 per cent in the South East. See W.H. Beveridge, 'An Analysis of Unemployment', *Economica*, N.S. III, 1936, pp.357–86.

31 This should not, of course, be taken to imply that rearmament was a smooth, straightforward process, but that the major obstacles were largely different from those faced by a public works programme. See, e.g., R. Shay, *British Rearmament in the Thirties*, 1977.

32 J.C.R. Dow, *The Management of the British Economy 1945–60*, Cambridge 1964, Chapter VII. See also Chapter 8 below.

33 K. Hancock, 'The Reduction of Unemployment as a Problem of Public Policy 1920–29', *Economic History Review*, XV, 1962, pp.328–43. The difficulties their inconsistent positions got the government into are illustrated by the fact that the Cabinet meeting which decided to publish the 1929 White Paper also discussed a draft election address including a reference to the government committing £400m to public works to help unemployment. This was eventually deleted because it seemed 'inconsistent with the Treasury contention that public works could only be carried out by taking money from the aggregated sum available for expenditure, and which would in any event have been used to give some employment', *Cabinet Conclusions* of 6 May 1929. P.R.O. CAB 23/60 20(29).

34 J.M. Keynes *Collected Writings* vol. IX, 1971, p.90 and p.91.

35 ibid., pp.109–10.

36 Committee on Finance and Industry: *Minutes of Evidence*, vol. II, Q5561–5710, 1932.

37 Winch, op. cit., p.121.

38 Committee on Finance and Industry, op. cit., Q5565.

39 ibid., Q5690.

40 ibid., Q5689.

41 *Hansard (Commons)*, 1928–29, vol. 227, column 54, 15 April 1929.

42 For details see R. Skidelsky, *Politicians and the Slump*, Harmondsworth, 1967, Chapter 8. R. Skidelsky, *Oswald Mosley*, 1975, Chapter 10.

43 He is not mentioned, though obviously relevant, in D. Mackay, D. Forsyth, D. Kelly, 'The discussion of public works programmes 1917–35: some remarks on the Labour Movement's constitution', *International Review of Social History*, XI, 1966.

44 Skidelsky, *Politicians and the Slump*, op. cit., pp.197-8.

45 See e.g. Mackay *et al.*, op. cit.

46 A.S. Blinder and R.M. Solow, 'Does Fiscal Policy Matter', *Journal of Public Economics*, 2, 1973.

47 *Memoranda on Certain Proposals*, op. cit., p.54.

48 Blinder and Solow, op. cit., p.321.

49 R. Harrod, *The Life of John Maynard Keynes*, 1952, p.405. S. Howson and D. Winch, *The Economic Advisory Council, 1930-39*, Cambridge, 1977, p.129.

50 J.M. Keynes, *Collected Writings*, vol. VI, 1971, Chapter 23.

51 *We Can Conquer Unemployment*, pp.54-5.

52 J.M. Keynes, *Collected Writings*, vol. VI, op. cit., p.8. Note that data on this question was not generally available at this time.

Chapter 6

1 In J.M. Keynes *Collected Writings*, vol. IX, 1972, p.212.

2 S. Pollard (ed.), *The Gold Standard and Employment Policies Between the Wars*, 1970, Introduction.

3 ibid., p.12.

4 Keynes, op. cit., pp.216, 218–19.

5 Pollard, op. cit., p.25.

6 ibid., pp.13–14.

7 D.E. Moggridge, *British Monetary Policy 1924-31: The Norman Conquest of $4.86*, Cambridge, 1972, p.233.

8 To take an extreme but not entirely absurd example, one could argue that the 1925 decision favoured the British working class. By provoking in part the general strike it formed new patterns of political alliances and practices which eventually were important to working-class interests. This is not entirely absurd given the Left's common view that economic

adversity produces political strength.

9 R.S. Sayers, *The Bank of England 1891–1914*, Cambridge, 1976, vol. I, pp. 99-109; H. Clay, *Lord Norman*, 1957, pp.101–3.

10 See Harvey's evidence in Committee on Finance and Industry (Macmillan Committee): *Minutes of Evidence* 1931, Q3.

11 Sayers, op. cit., vol. I, p.110. Also Moggridge, op. cit., p.145.

12 For example, F. Hirsch and P. Oppenheimer, 'The trial of managed money: currency credit and prices 1920–70 in C. Cipolla (ed.), *The Fontana Economic History of Europe: The Twentieth Century*, 1976.

13 T. Balogh, *Studies in Financial Organisation*, Cambridge, 1947, p.191.

14 Sayers, op. cit., vol. I, p.113.

15 E.V. Morgan, *Studies in British Financial Policy 1914–1925*, 1952, p.143.

16 PRO CAB 23/60 5(29). The autonomy of the Bank was defended at the 1930 Labour Party Conference by Snowden. S. Howson and D. Winch, *The Economic Advisory Council 1930–1939*, Cambridge, 1977, p.26.

17 Moggridge, op. cit., p.96.

18 ibid., p.242.

19 J.M. Keynes, *Tract on Monetary Reform, Collected Writings*, vol. IV, 1971; *The Economic Consequences of Mr Churchill, Collected Writings* IX, 1972. A similar kind of argument is used by R.G. Hawtrey, *Monetary Reconstruction*, 1923, Chapter 3 which discusses the gold standard starting with an analysis of changes in the value of money on debts.

20 Sayers, op. cit., vol. I, p.135n.

21 J. Clapham, G. Guillebaud, F. Lavington, D. Robertson, *Monetary Policy: Report of a British Association Sub-Committee on Currency and the Gold Standard*, 1921.

22 *Papers Relating to the International Economic Conference Genoa April–May 1922*, CMD. 1667, Parliamentary Papers 1922, XXIII.

23 Moggridge, op. cit., p.92 and Appendix 2.

24 D. Williams, 'Montagu Norman and banking policy in the 1920s', *Yorkshire Bulletin* II, 1 July 1959, pp.51, 54.

25 R.S. Sayers, 'The Return to Gold, 1925' in Pollard (ed.), op. cit.

26 For example even if British exports were price elastic, could a lower value of the pound have been made effective in major markets? For one case see J. Tomlinson, 'The Pound/Rupee Exchange in the 1920s', *Indian Economic and Social History Review*, XV, 2, April–June 1978.

27 Pollard (ed.), op. cit., p.23.

28 S. Howson, *Domestic Monetary Management in Britain 1919–1938*, Cambridge, 1975.

29 In the next few paragraphs I draw upon an unpublished paper by A. Hussain, an extended review of Howson, op. cit.

30 Howson, op. cit., p.1. See also p.28.

31 Moggridge, op. cit., p.142.

32 Macmillan Committee, op. cit., Q5548–9.

33 Howson, op. cit., p.36.

34 W.A. Brown, *The International Gold Standard Re-interpreted*, New York, 1940, vol. I, p.670.

35 ibid., vol. I, p.155.

36 Howson, op. cit., p.41.

37 D. Williams, 'London and the 1931 financial crisis', *Economic History Review*, XV, 3, 1962–63.

38 P. Einzig, *Montagu Norman*, 1932, p.42.

39 L.S. Pressnell, '1925: the burden of sterling', *Economic History Review* XXXI, 1, 1978. Also W.A. Brown, *England and the New Gold Standard*, 1929, p.263.

40 Pollard (ed.), op. cit., p.14.

41 Macmillan Committee, op. cit., Q7079–219.

42 ibid., Q7100.

43 S. Pollard, 'The nationalisation of the banks: the chequered history of a socialist proposal', in D. Martin and D. Rubenstein, *Ideology and the Labour Movement*, 1978.

44 For example, J.M. Keynes, 'The Monetary Policy of the Labour Party', *New Statesman*, 17 and 24 September 1932.

Chapter 7

1 N. Mansergh, *The Commonwealth Experience*, 1969, p.163; I.M. Drummond, *Imperial Economic Policy 1917–1939*, 1974, p.426.

2 Though as an exception see Economic Advisory Council, Committee on Empire Migration *Report*, CMD. 4075, Parliamentary Papers, 1931–2 IX.

3 D. Winch, *Economics and Policy*, 1969.

4 Drummond, op. cit., and *British Economic Policy and the Empire, 1919–1939*, 1972.

5 Lenin's *Imperialism the Highest Stage of Capitalism*, Collected Works vol. XXX is far from being a theoretical text. It is a political polemic, in the course of which Lenin marshalls all kinds of heterogeneous and even contradictory elements to drive his political points home. For a corrective to the constant distortions of the work see E.T. Stokes, 'Late nineteenth century expansion and the attack on the theory of Economic Imperialism', *Historical Journal*, XII, 1969.

6 *Paris Resolutions of 1916*, CMD. 8271, Parliamentary Papers, 1916 XXXIV, Resolution B III.

7 Thus one of the most sustained (and unsuccessful) attempts at Empire self-sufficiency was launched in the case of cotton growing — large funds going to the Empire Cotton-Growing Committee. See *Report on the*

Board of Trade of the Empire Cotton-Growing Committee, Parliamentary Papers 1920, XVI and the issues of the *Empire Cotton-Growing Review*, founded 1924.

8 *Final Report of the Committee on Commercial and Industrial Policy After the War* (Balfour Committee) Cd. 9035, Parliamentary Papers, 1918 XIII.

9 House of Commons *Debates* LXXIV, vol. 22, col. 1964, 21 September 1915.

10 E.V. Morgan, *British Financial Policy 1914–1925*, 1952, Table 5, p.98. For comparison National Income in Britain in 1913 was probably a little over £2000m.

11 A. Peacock and J. Wiseman, *The Growth of Public Expenditure in the United Kingdom*, 2nd edn, 1967, especially pp.24–8.

12 This calculation by the Treasury was perfectly sensible given the terms in which it operated. This point is made strongly by Athar Hussain in an unpublished review of S. Howson's *Domestic Monetary Management in Britain 1919–38*, Cambridge, 1975.

13 B. Mallet and C.O. George, *British Budgets 1921–22 to 1932–33*, 1933, Appendix, Table XVIII.

14 *Report of Committee appointed to consider the measures to be taken for settling within the Empire ex-servicemen who may desire to emigrate after the war* (Tennyson Committee) Cd. 8672, Parliamentary Papers 1917–18 X, para. 5.

15 W.K. Hancock, *Survey of Commonwealth Affairs II Problems of Economic Policy 1918–1939*, Part 2, Oxford, 1940, p.130.

16 Quoted in *Report of Overseas Settlement Committee for 1928*, Cmd. 3308, P.P. 1928–9 VIII, p.5. See also Amery, *Empire and Prosperity*, 1930, p.51; Milner quoted in W.A. Carrothers, *Emigration from the British Isles*, 1929, pp.260–1.

17 For example J.A. Schultz, 'Canadian attitudes towards Empire settlement', *Journal of Imperial and Commonwealth History*, I, 2 January 1973.

18 *Extracts from the Proceedings laid before the Imperial War Conference 1917*, Cd. 8566, P.P. 1917–18 XXIII, p.114.

19 Drummond, *Imperial Economic Policy*, op. cit., p.136.

20 ibid., pp.71–2.

21 J.M. Atkin, 'Official Regulation of British Overseas Investment, 1914–1931', *Economic History Review* XXIII, 2, 1970.

22 ibid.

23 *Report of the Overseas Settlement Commitment for 1928*, CMD. 3308, Parliamentary Papers 1929, VIII, p.5.

24 A.J.P. Taylor, *Beaverbrook*, Harmondsworth, 1974, p.221.

25 W.A.S. Hewins, *Apologia of an Imperialist*, 1929, vol. II, p.266.

26 'Free trade, preference and migration', *Round Table*, no. 52, September 1923.

27 J. Amery, *The Life of Joseph Chamberlain*, 1969, vol. VI, p.1015.

28 In 1930 only 17 per cent of British imports were subject to tariffs, J.H. Richardson, *British Economic Foreign Policy*, 1936, p.90.

29 Committee on Finance and Industry *Report*, Cmd. 3897, P.P. 1930–31 XIII, Addendum I.

30 House of Commons *Debates*, vol. 261, Cols. 280–96, 4 February 1932.

31 L.S. Amery, *Empire and Prosperity*, 1930, p.29.

32 S. Howson and D. Winch, *The Economic Advisory Council 1930–39*, Cambridge, 1977, pp.99–100.

33 J. Amery, op. cit., p.1026.

34 W.A.S. Hewins, *Trade in the Balance*, 1924, pp.91–5.

35 Drummond, *Imperial Economic Policy*, op. cit., p.433.

36 Drummond, *British Economic Policy and the Empire*, op. cit., p.114.

37 C.R. Fay, *Imperial Economy*, 1934, pp.141–2.

38 L.S. Amery, *National and Imperial Economics*, 1924, p.60.

Chapter 8

1 R.C.O. Matthews, 'Why has Britain had full employment since the War?', *Economic Journal*, 78, 3, 1968. The approach of this chapter to some degree parallels H. Stein, *The Fiscal Revolution in America*, Chicago, 1968.

2 Current Account of Central Government Including National Insurance Funds, *Financial Statistics*, H.M.S.O. Other government statistics, *Economic Trends* for example, sometimes give a date even later in the 1970s.

3 M. Stewart, *Keynes and After*, 1967, p.9.

4 R. Lekachman, *The Age of Keynes*, 1969, Chapter 11.

5 J.M. Buchanan *et al.*, *The Consequences of Mr. Keynes*, Hobart Papers 78, I.E.A., 1978.

6 D. Winch, *Economics and Policy*, 1972.

7 S. Howson and D. Winch, *The Economic Advisory Council 1930–39*, Cambridge, 1977.

8 ibid, pp.151–2.

9 S. Howson, *Domestic Monetary Management in Britain 1919–38*, Cambridge, 1975.

10 ibid., p.143.

11 Cf. A. Cutler *et al.*, *Marx's Capital and Capitalism Today*, 1978, vol. II, pp.40–1.

12 After the restoration of gold in 1925 there were sterling crises in 1927 (following the general strike); 1929 (following the Wall Street boom); and

of course the final one of 1931.

13 J.M. Keynes, 'Alternative Aims in Monetary Policy' in *Essays in Persuasion*, Collected Writings, vol. IX, 1971, p.179.

14 Para. 168.

15 Howson, op. cit., pp.47–54.

16 E. Nevin, *The Mechanism of Cheap Money*, Cardiff, 1955, p.109.

17 A. Marwick, 'Middle opinion in the 30s: planning progress and political agreement', *English Historical Review*, 79, 1964.

18 Cf. D.H. Aldcroft, 'The development of the managed economy before 1939', *Journal of Contemporary History*, 4, 4, 1969.

19 E. Carry Brown, 'Fiscal policy in the 'thirties: a reappraisal', *American Economic Review*, XLVI, 2, 1956.

20 A. Peacock and J. Wiseman, *The Growth of Public Expenditure in the U.K.*, 2nd edn., 1967, Chapter 3. These figures are for all government expenditure (central and local) in relation to GNP at factor cost in current prices.

21 R.M. Bird: '"Wagner's Law" of Expanding State Activity', *Public Finance*, XXVI, 1, 1971.

22 G. Thompson, *Theories of the Growth of the Public Sector*, Open University Course D323, Block 1, Unit 3 1979.

23 Peacock and Wiseman, op. cit.

24 R.M. Bird, *The growth of Government Spending in Canada*, Toronto, 1970, pp.107–16 and F.L. Pryor, *Public Expenditure in Communist and Capitalist Nations*, 1968, Appendix E–3.

25 M. Abramowitz and V. Eliasberg, *The Growth of Public Employment in Great Britain*, NBER, Princeton, 1957, pp.83–4.

26 J. Wiseman 'Local Government in the Twentieth Century', *Lloyds Bank Review*, 79, 1966.

27 J.C.R. Dow, *The Management of the British Economy 1945–60*, Cambridge, 1965, Chapters 7 and 8.

28 B.E.V. Sabine, *British Budgets in Peace and War 1932–45*, 1970, p.297.

29 R.S. Sayers, *Financial Policy 1939–45*, 1956, pp.99-111.

30 For histories of National Income accounting see P. Studenski, *The Income of Nations*, New York, 1958 and J.W. Kendrick, 'The historical development of National Income accounts', *History of Political Economy*, 2, 3, 1970.

31 D. Patinkin, 'Keynes and econometrics', *Econometrica*, 44, 6, 1976, pp.1116–18.

32 A. Flux, 'The National Income', *Journal of the Royal Statistical Society*, XCII, 1, 1929, p.7.

33 D. Seers, 'The political economy of National Accounting' in A. Cairncross and M. Pur (eds.), *Employment, Income Distribution and Development Strategy*, 1976.

34 C.S. Carson, 'The history of US National Income and Product accounts:

the devleopment of an analytical tool', *Review of Income and Wealth*, Series 21, 1975.

35 ibid., p.161.

36 Op. cit., p.1104.

37 Seers, op. cit., p.194. This is not meant to imply that National Income estimates are simply an elaboration of neoclassical or any other theory. All kinds of other (non-theoretical) exigencies enter into their calculation. Indeed it could well be argued that Kuznets's position (e.g. the exclusion of many governmental services from calculations of final product) in the late forties was *more* consistently neoclassical than the general international measures used today. See his 'Government Product and National Income' in E. Lundert (ed.), *Income and Wealth*, Series I, Cambridge, 1951. Of course particular aspects of modern National Income accounting can be seen as essentially Keynesian e.g. treatment of fixed capital formation as inherently distinct from other types of expenditure.

38 A.E. Feaveryear, 'Spending the National Income', *Economic Journal*, XLI, No. 161.

39 R. Stone, 'The use and development of National Income and Expenditure estimates' in D.N. Chester (ed.), *Lessons of the British War Economy*, Cambridge, 1951.

40 G. Colm, 'Experience in the use of social accounting in public policy in the US', in Lundbert (ed.), op. cit., pp.77–8. See also Carson, op. cit., pp.165–6 and Temporary National Economic Committee, *Hearings*, Part 9, USGPO, pp.3520–38.

41 *An Analysis of the Sources of War Finance and an Estimate of the National Income and Expenditure in 1938 and 1940*, CMD. 6261, Parliamentary Papers, 1940–41, VIII.

42 Sayers, op. cit., chapters 2–4.

43 Quoted in Keynes, *Collected Writings*, vol. XXII, 1978, p.107.

44 Stein, op. cit., p.174.

45 R.M. Titmuss, *Essays on the Welfare State*, 1963, p.82.

46 J. Harris, *William Beveridge: A Biography*, Oxford, 1977, Chapter 17.

47 P. Addison, *The Road to 1945*, 1975.

48 ibid., p.242.

49 Harris, op. cit., pp.428–34.

50 D. Winch, *Economics and Policy*, 1972, pp.279–84.

Index

Subject index